THE ORDER OF MELCHIZEDEK

A REVELATION OF THE KING/PRIEST MINISTRY

SHEDDING LIGHT UPON ONE OF THE MOST MISUNDERSTOOD YET PROFOUND TRUTHS OF HOLY SCRIPTURE

THE ORDER OF MELCHIZEDEK

CHARLES A. JENNINGS

TRUTH IN HISTORY

OWASSO, OKLAHOMA

The Order of Melchizedek
Charles A. Jennings
Truth in History
© Copyright 2010, 2018 All Rights Reserved.
Cataloging information
ISBN-10 0-9829817-0-8
ISBN-13 978-0-9829817-0-2

Table of Contents

APPENDIXES

Acknowledgements

Acknowledgement and thanks to my wife for her long hours of transcribing the original audio sermons and many hours of computer work. Without her assistance and patience this book would not exist; and to Eleanor McCutchen, a true mother of Israel, for reading my manuscript and her many helpful suggestions, encouragement and inspiration.

Charles A. Jennings

Who was Melchizedek?

In my early research into this topic some years ago I began to see the impact and importance of this wonderful subject. As Christians we should be constantly learning the purpose and ways of God, to the day we die. However, sometimes 'church' can be one of the greatest hindrances to our knowledge of God. We can become locked into a church system that becomes stagnant. The church brought you to God, but it can also become a means by which it keeps you from a deeper knowledge of Him. That can apply to a local church, a denomination, or any one of the historical churches that we have all encountered. The leaders may build a *memorial* to a great revival which took place in the past, then build a *monument* which becomes a *mausoleum*. Therefore, the church can become nothing but a *mortuary*.

We can go through sincere religious exercises, but ten different times the Lord told Moses (and Moses told Pharaoh,) *"Let my people go,"*—and for what reason? *"That they may serve me."* Not just for a miracle to take place, which was wonderful and great, but that they may serve Me. The emphasis therefore is upon the person of God. The Red Sea experience was just a one-time experience, but the serving is to be continual. Every major thing that God does is a means whereby He reveals Himself, by the use of another sacred name such as Jireh, Tsidkeenu, Mekaddishken, and so forth. He wants to reveal Himself to us by His Word. Of all the wonderful ideas and events that we find in the Bible, the **order of Melchizedek** is the most neglected. It is very seldom, if ever mentioned, even then with confusion.

The first scriptural record of Melchizedek is found in Genesis 14. Who was Melchizedek. What was his ministry. What did he do. Is he still alive? Genesis 14 contains a description of the first recorded war in the Bible. Abram and his nephew Lot had split from one another. They decided the land would not support all of their flocks and herds, so they went their separate ways. Lot chose the fertile valley of the plain which included the cities of Sodom, Gomorrah, Zoar and others. Lot was living in Sodom and Abram was living on the plains of Mamre. Five kings invaded the valley where Lot had settled and took loot from the city of Sodom and other cities. They took captive women, children, and Lot himself.

Genesis 14:10-14 reads, *"And the vale of Siddim was full of slimepits; and the kings of Sodom and Gomorrah fled, and fell there; and they that remained fled to the mountain. And they took all the goods of Sodom and Gomorrah, and all their victuals and went their way. And they took Lot, Abram's brother's son, who dwelt in Sodom and departed."* [Lot shouldn't have been there in the first place, but he was there] *"And there came one that had escaped and told Abram the Hebrew, for he dwelt in the plain of Mamre the Amorite, the brother of Eshcol, and brother of Aner: and these were confederate with Abram. And when Abram heard that his brother* [brother's son] *was taken captive, he armed his trained servants, born in his own house, three hundred and eighteen, and pursued them unto Dan."*

On one side there were five kings and their armies. On the other there was Abram and three hundred and eighteen of his warriors. Three hundred and nineteen men on one side and five nations on the other." *And he divided himself against them ..."* Abram put half of his men on one side and half on the other side.

"...he and his servants by night and smote them, and pursued them unto Hobah, which is on the left hand of Damascus. And he brought back all the goods and also brought again his brother [nephew] Lot, and his goods, and the women also, and the people. And the king of Sodom went out to meet him after his return from the slaughter of Chedorlaomer, and of the kings that were with him, at the valley of Shaveh, which is the king's dale." The king of Sodom came out to meet Abram and to offer his gratitude. *"And Melchizedek, King of Salem, brought forth bread and wine: and he was the priest of the most high God."* Gen. 14:15-18

Seemingly, out of nowhere, Abram met a man known as the priest of the most high God and the king of a city. The city of Salem was the old name of the city of Jerusalem. Salem means peace. *"And he blessed him and said, Blessed be Abram of the most high God, possessor of heaven and earth; And blessed be the most high God which hath delivered thine enemies into thy hand. And he gave him tithes of all."* (Gen. 14:18-20). Melchizedek blessed Abram and Abram gave him the tithes of all the loot and the goods that he had taken from this recent war. Abram gave Melchizedek the tithes and Melchizedek gave Abram two things: a blessing and a serving of bread and wine. Melchizedek said, "Blessed be Abram ... possessor of heaven and earth." Who is Melchizedek referring to as being the possessor of heaven and earth. God, Abram or both. It would be safe to say both, because we know that God is the possessor of heaven and earth. Melchizedek was a priest, and a king. He had some knowledge that this man whom he was blessing, and his seed were going to be the possessors of heaven and earth.

Later we see the confirmation of this Abrahamic covenant. When God said Abram's seed shall be as the sand of the seashore and the stars of heaven, Abram became the possessor of heaven and earth. *"And he blessed him and said, Blessed be Abram of* [and by] *the most high God, possessor of heaven and earth and blessed be the most high God."* In verse 19 is the blessing on Abram and in verse 20, Melchizedek is blessing the most high God. *"And blessed be the most high God that hath delivered thine enemies into thine hand. And he gave him tithes of all."* Concerning the king of Sodom we read, *"The king of Sodom said unto Abram, Give me the persons, and take the goods to thyself. And Abram said to the king of Sodom, I have lift up mine hand unto the Lord, the most high God, the possessor of heaven and earth that I will not take from a thread even to the shoelachet, and that I will not take anything that is thine, lest thou shouldest say, I have made Abram rich: Save only that which the young men have eaten, and the portion of the men which went with me… let them take their portion."* Gen. 14:21-24

SHEM

Questions have always been raised as to who this man Melchizedek was. The term Melchizedek does not refer to a certain man, but rather refers to an office. An office is always conferred upon a man. A president is not a president until that office is conferred upon him. **'Melchizedek' was an office and the man himself was Shem.** Now the only other possible viable answer that has been put forth by many teachers is that Melchizedek was a theophany or an appearance of Jesus Christ before His physical birth. In order to understand this whole concept we must recognize the man himself was Shem. *(See Appendix Charts)*

From the charts we will see that it was very possible for Shem to have been Melchizedek, because when this incident took place in Genesis 14, Shem was still alive. In Genesis 11, Shem was 100 years old when his son Arphaxad was born and Arphaxad's son was born when Arphaxad was 35 years old. Continuing on to Abraham's father, in Genesis 11:16, Terah lived 70 years and begat Abram, Nahor and Haran. In adding these figures, it comes to 390 years. So we have 390 years from the time Shem's son was born until the birth of Abram. Then Shem lived another 210 years, which totals 600 years. Abram lived only 175 years. Therefore Shem outlived Abram by 35 years.

The Bible tells us in Genesis 11 that Shem lived 98 years before the flood. Abram was 75 years old when God called him in Genesis 12. He lived 100 years after that, for a total of 175 years, and Shem was still living at that time. Isaac was born when his father Abram was 100 years old. Isaac's son Jacob was born when Abram was 160 years old. Since Abraham died at 175, that means Jacob was 15 years old when his grandfather died. Jacob was 50 years old (take the 15 and add the 35 years that Shem was still living after the death of Abram), which means Isaac was 110 years old when Shem died, while Jacob was 50 years old. Abram's son and grandson were alive when their eleventh generation grandfather was still living. There were eleven generations still living at the same time. Shem was still alive when his eleventh generation grandson, Jacob, was born. Therefore, it is physically possible that Shem was still alive when Abram fought this war. Shem was the one who came out of the city of Salem, met him, blessed him and gave him bread and wine. We note that throughout the history of Samuel, the Kings and Chronicles. Scripture talks about the city of Jerusalem being a holy city; the city where God had placed His name. It did not start with David, because Salem was the old name for that same city. This man, who held this dual office of King- Priest, was already residing in this city of Salem. This meeting takes place, but very little material concerning it is found throughout the Old Testament.

(See Appendix – Who was Melchizedek? Page A-2)

NOAH'S OATHS

Shem was definitely mentioned in Noah's blessing of the Lord in Genesis 9:24. The scriptural record does not contain a lot of detail, but enough to let us know that Shem received a blessing. *"And Noah awoke from his wine and he knew what his younger son had done unto him. And he said, Cursed be Canaan;* [Ham's son] *a servant of servants shall he be unto his brethren. Blessed be the Lord God of Shem; and Canaan shall be his servant. God shall enlarge Japheth, and Canaan shall be his servant."* There were three sons. Ham was the younger. The other son Japheth is a lesser son even though he is the oldest, because Noah said that Japheth is going to dwell in the tents of his younger brother Shem. Shem is the one who received this blessing in verse 26 when it said, *"Blessed be the Lord God of Shem."* Herein is a correlation with the words of Melchizedek in Genesis 14, when he blessed the Lord and Noah also blessed the Lord. In Hebrew patriarchal culture, the patriarch of that race and family was both its civil and spiritual leader. He had the authority to confer blessings and cursings upon his sons. Whatever that curse was, it worked upon Canaan. In effect he said, 'Japheth, you are going to follow your brother Shem.' Then he said; 'Blessed *be the Lord God of Shem.'* He connected Shem with righteousness and with the Lord God.

Being that Shem was Melchizedek, where and how did he receive this dual office of King-Priest. He received it from Noah, who held it before him. The Bible doesn't specifically say that Noah was Melchizedek, nor where and when this order started. It doesn't say who the first Melchizedek was, but Noah, who was the patriarchal father of his race at the time, conferred this dual office upon his son Shem, as recorded in Gen. 9:26.

How did these men receive this dual office. *It was only by oath.* It had to be spoken out of the mouth of someone who had the authority to speak and confer that office. It could not be done by just anyone; it had to be conferred by a predecessor in that same line. Shem was definitely mentioned in Noah's blessing in Gen. 9:26, and this passage therefore implies that Shem was a devout and Godly man and consequently deserved to have this blessing upon him. Shem was his earthly name; Melchizedek was his priestly and kingly name. Later on in the Bible we find the tribe of Judah was appointed as the royal tribe of Israel, the tribe of Israel's kings. The tribe of Levi was appointed to take care of all the spiritual matters, priestly functions and upkeep of the tabernacle. Each served in their own capacity. Kings did not meddle in the affairs of the priests and priests did not meddle in the affairs of the king. Melchizedek held both offices and functioned in both roles.

Basically, there are only three offices in the Old Testament: prophet, priest and king. *Prophets* officiated at the door of the temple or at the gate of the city and their message was, *'Thus saith the Lord.'* They rebuked the people and gave promise of a coming invasion, or a promise of hope, but they did not serve at the altar. The *priests* filled their role at the altar and were to make sacrifices for the sins of the people. A bloody mess resulted where they made the sacrifices, sprinkled blood, poured out sacrifices of wine and meal offerings, and brought the meat offerings. All that ceremony had to be observed according to the prescribed order. The temple was in the center of Hebrew and Israelite society. Then there was the **king** who sat on the throne. He gave the orders. The king had the authority to say, 'let's go to war,' and he could muster the army to defend a city and could make civil decisions.

This Melchizedek order was established before the Mosaic order and existed many years before Moses was born. Who established this order. When was it established. Which was the greater order—the Melchizedek or the Mosaic order. Which was eternal. Which one expired. The Levitical order expired. The Melchizedek order was *"without mother or father"* and without ending of days, according to Hebrews 7. A mystery surrounds this order, but it is fulfilled in a **person** who still holds the office. We know more about the **present order** of Melchizedek than we do about the **origin** of the order of Melchizedek. This study of Melchizedek will bring a greater vision of the ministry of Jesus Christ and who He was and is today. All prophecy and history is consummated in Him. He fulfilled the Levitical order and brought it to a close. He then brought to fruition the continuing effect of the Melchizedek order which is unending.

JESUS AND MELCHIZEDEK

Similarities between Melchizedek and Christ are apparent. **1)** Neither one was of the Tribe of Levi, yet both had a continuing priesthood. **2)** Both were appointed priests *by oath* and not by the law of commandment or ancestral descent as were the Levitical priests. The Melchizedek priesthood was the order already in place for which Christ had to meet the requirements or qualifications or otherwise He was not *'after the order of.'* For instance, like being president of the United States, there are certain requirements. You have to be native born, of minimum age and have certain physical requirements. The president may have been born in 1950, but the office existed long before he was ever born. The office of Melchizedek existed before Jesus was born. He had to meet the qualifications of that office, or He would not have been *'after the order of'* Melchizedek. If He did not meet those qualifications, He would have been establishing a brand new order of priesthood.

In John 8:55-57 we have a glimpse of what Jesus was saying when He said, *"Yet ye have not known him: but I know him: and if I should say, I know him not, I shall be a liar like unto you: but I know him, and keep his saying. Your father Abraham rejoiced to see my day: and he saw it, and was glad. Then said the Jews unto him, thou art not yet fifty years old and hast thou seen Abraham. Jesus said unto them, Verily, verily I say unto you, before Abraham was, I am."* The Jews had enough sense to know that this man in His physical body was less than fifty years old, yet He made the statement, 'I AM', enraging the Jews by appropriating one of the holiest Names of God. Not 'I was', but I AM before Abraham. His function, office, anointing and very being existed long before Abraham. Jesus was less than fifty years old in the flesh, but His ministry began long before Bethlehem.

Abraham saw the Lord's Day two different times. The first time was described in Gen. 14. The second time Abraham saw the Lord's Day is found in Gen. 18. It says, *"And the LORD* [all caps, which denotes the personal name of God Himself] *appeared unto him in the plains of Mamre; and he sat in the tent door in the heat of the day. And he lifted up his eyes and looked and lo three men stood by him and when he saw them, he ran to meet them from the tent door, and bowed himself toward the ground."* Verse 13 says, *"And the LORD said unto Abraham..."* The Lord Himself spoke to Abraham. Verse 16 goes on: *"And the men rose up from thence: and looked toward Sodom: and Abraham went with them to bring them on the way. And the LORD said, shall I hide from Abraham that thing which I do?.* Verse 22. *"And the men turned their faces from thence."* What men. The men referred to in verse 16, but only two of these men. There had been three men who first appeared to Abraham as he sat in his tent, but only two men went down to Sodom. *"And the men turned their faces from thence, and went toward Sodom: but Abraham stood yet before the LORD."*

In other words, Jesus Christ stood there before Abraham, but He sent the two angels down to Sodom to evaluate the situation. This number 'two' is very significant, because it's by the testimony of two or three witnesses that sufficient evidence is established in the Mosaic legal system. We see when Jesus was on the Mount of Transfiguration, He had two witnesses with Him, Moses and Elijah. Then He had the three earthly witnesses, Peter, James and John. At His resurrection and at His ascension, He had two witnesses. (See Luke 24:4 and Acts 1:10)

There were two highly respected institutions which governed Hebrew culture. They were *1)* fatherhood, and *2)* spiritual priesthood. Hebrew culture was a patriarchal society. It was not matriarchal. The women were valued very highly, but their role did not encompass matters of governance. The following women evidenced the Spirit of God in their ministry, such as Deborah, Ruth, Hulda the prophetess, and other women, but they were living within the confines and under the headship of a patriarchal order. I do not demean women at all, but one of the signs of the times in which we live, indicating 'the end of the age,' is women having an unprecedented authority in culture and society. Perverted Christianity is pushing them to the forefront. Women are assuming roles of leadership in Bible teaching and preaching. The men are now following them and are not taking their God-ordained lead in determining doctrine and practice. They are turning this over as a **transfer of power** to women.

In the area of *fatherhood*, the oldest living patriarch of the Adamic race at any time was considered to be the civil authority. In the Old Testament there was that spiritual office of fatherhood and the father was the head of that family. At any given time the oldest patriarch living in the Hebrew family was the spiritual head of the family. Noah said, 'Ham, your offspring is cursed' and it was so. He said, 'Shem, blessed be the Lord God of Shem' and it was so. He said, 'Japheth, you are going to dwell in the tents of Shem.'

The second was *priesthood.* The oldest living patriarch of the Adamic race at any given time was considered to be the religious authority or the priest of his race. In the upside down world that we live in, parents have lost control and children are now dictating what and where to eat, what to wear, what not to wear, where and when to go to church, and indeed, if anyone goes at all. Then we must consider the school system. Now we have policemen in the school buildings to keep the students in order. What kind of a society are we living in. Where are our fathers and what role are they playing in their families and in the wider community?

The Book of Hebrews contains the principles of the Levitical and Melchizedek priesthoods, in contrasting the two. In Hebrews 6: 4-6 the writer says, *"for it is impossible for those who were once enlightened, and have tasted of the heavenly gift, and were made partakers of the Holy Ghost, And have tasted the good word of God, and the powers of the world to come, if they shall fall away,* [in the Greek the word is apostatize, it is impossible] *to renew them again unto repentance."* The word 'repentance' itself gives us a connection with sacrifice. Why did the writer of Hebrews put this thought here when he is talking about priesthood. We have the Melchizedek priesthood that has been in existence for thousands of years before Moses came along, and through the inspiration of God Himself, Moses institutes another priesthood called the Levitical priesthood. Then Jesus Christ comes and fulfills the Levitical priesthood and it came to an end. In the early church, Judaizers said, 'Yes, we believe in the grace of God, BUT you have to be circumcised." The writer of Hebrews is setting forth the fact that the Levitical order of the Old Testament has been fulfilled. They were then, in the first century, living in the Melchizedek priesthood and the writer was telling his readers, if you who have now tasted of the good gift of God, and the powers of the world to come, then revert back to Judaism, there is no hope for you. If you revert back to the old structure of the Levitical order in the Old Testament, there is no hope for salvation. To apostatize means to do disgrace to the present Melchizedek order and revert back to the old Levitical order of which Judaism today is a perversion of that old ceremonial system.

Christians who are now advocating blood sacrifice of animals as part of Jewish worship are an affront to the Melchizedek Priesthood. The red heifer that some Christians in America are trying to breed is being done in order to export it to Palestine. Then they can maintain, 'we have a perfect animal for sacrifices.' Its perfect offspring must be born in Palestine, to fulfill the old order. The writer of Hebrews is telling us that the Levitical order has been abolished. Now the superior and greater priesthood, called the Melchizedek order, is in effect. It is a more excellent way. In the book of Hebrews, Christ is shown to be better than the prophets, the angels, Moses, Joshua, the High Priest and Abraham. Now there is a better way, a better hope, a better covenant, a better promise, a better sacrifice, a better substance, a better country, a better resurrection and better things.

TWO IMMUTABLE THINGS

In Hebrews 6:6 & 10 it says, *"If they shall fall away,* [if they should apostatize and go back to the old priesthood] *it is impossible ... to renew them again unto repentance, seeing they crucify to themselves the Son of God afresh,* [over and over again] *and put him to an open shame." "For God is not unrighteous to forget your work and labour of love, which ye have shown toward his name, in that ye have ministered to the saints and do minister."* This ministering that is mentioned in verse ten is not the Levitical ministry, it is the Melchizedek ministry to saints. Who are the saints. How did Melchizedek minister to Abram. He served him two things: bread and wine. What did Jesus serve. Bread and wine. What did He say in chapter six, verse 53 of John. *"Unless ye eat my flesh and drink my blood you have no life in you."* He is here to give of Himself. He said, *"eat my flesh and drink my blood."* That was the greater communion. What He served the twelve apostles at the last supper was only a token of His full communion. In John six, He stressed if you continue to eat My flesh and continue to drink My blood, then you have life in you.

In Hebrews 6:11-12 it says, *"And we desire that every one of you do show the same diligence to the full assurance of hope unto the end. That ye be not slothful, but followers of them who through faith and patience inherit the promises."* Who are the 'them' referred to in this verse. *"For when God made promises to Abraham, because he could swear by no greater, he swore by himself."* Follow the faith of Abraham. In Hebrews 6:13, God gave this promise to Abraham by an **oath**. *"And the angel of the LORD called unto Abraham out of heaven the second time, and said, **by myself have I sworn ...**"* This is what the writer of Hebrews is talking about when God made promise, because He could swear by no greater, He swear by Himself. *"By myself have I sworn, saith the LORD"* Genesis 22:16.

The Abrahamic covenant came by a divine oath. Who is going to disannul or has the power to rescind that? Nobody. Who would even think of changing the purpose of God, except perhaps theologians. "The Abrahamic covenant is gone. It is over with," say the theologians. What are they doing when they say that. They are calling God a liar. He said "by Myself." What is God doing. He is swearing by His own existence and His own integrity. By all of His wonderful immutable attributes He is saying, "I am putting My verity on the line. I am putting My faithfulness on the line. I am risking My ability to execute that which has gone out of my mouth." *"Saying, Surely blessing I will bless thee, and multiplying I will multiply* thee. *And so after he had patiently endured, he obtained the promise"* (Hebrews 6:14-15). What was the promise. Isaac was the fulfillment of the promise.

Genesis 22 contains the account of God testing Abraham's faith. He commanded him to sacrifice Isaac, who was Abraham's only legitimate child, the one from whom God had promised He would make Abraham a great nation, with descendants as numerous as the grains of sand by the sea. Now God was telling him to sacrifice this only son. Isaac himself was confused. *"Father,"* he said, *"behold* [here is] *the fire and the wood, but where is the lamb for a burnt offering?"* Across the ages, Abraham's statement of faith echoes down to encourage us: *"My son, God will provide Himself a lamb for a burnt offering."* Abraham turned and saw a ram caught in the thicket, which became the sacrifice in place of Isaac. The sacrifice of the blood was made for the promised son and his seed. It was a covenantal offering. That is why the **intent** of the death of Jesus Christ was for atonement of Isaac and his seed. The **extent** is to bless all creation. Isaac got down off the altar, and was spared. We were also spared because we are of Isaac's seed.

In Hebrews 6:16 it says, *"For men verily swear by the greater: and an oath for confirmation is to them an end of all strife"* [dispute]. That is the end, there is no more argument. *"Wherein God, willing more abundantly to show unto the heirs of promise the immutability of his counsel, confirmed it by an oath"* (Hebrews 6:17). By His attribute of immutability in His character, His purpose was confirmed by an oath in the Abrahamic covenant. *"That by two immutable things,* [*so* far only <u>one</u> thing is mentioned and that is the Abrahamic covenant] *in which it was impossible for God to lie, we might have a strong consolation,* [confidence] *who have fled for refuge to lay hold upon the hope set before us"* (Hebrews 6:18). What He is saying to us is that there is hope in the Abrahamic covenant. Because God swore, you can put your hope in the Abrahamic covenant. *"Which hope we have as an anchor of the soul, both sure and steadfast, and which entereth into that within the veil; whither the forerunner is for us entered, even Jesus, made a. high priest for ever after the order of Melchizedek.* (Hebrews 6:19-20). There are two things between verses 13 and 20 that were given by oath. They were the **Abrahamic covenant** and the **Melchizedek King/ Priest Order**.

David records in Psalm 110:4: *"The LORD hath sworn, and will not repent,* [change His mind] *Thou art a priest for ever after the order of Melchizedek."* So there are two things are recorded in Hebrews six that God set in order **by an oath**. These are the two immutable things in which it is impossible for God to lie. The Abrahamic covenant and a Melchizedek priesthood are in existence today. He did not mention the Levitical priesthood.

The writer says in Hebrews 6:16 that those two immutable things settle all disputes. In verse 17 they are described as unchangeable. These are His counsel, or God's purpose. In verse 18 they give us strong consolation or comfort and in verse 19 they anchor the soul. They are the anchor of our hope. You can place your faith deep into these two things; the Abrahamic covenant and the Melchizedek priesthood, fulfilled in Jesus Christ our Savior. He took the penalty of sin for Isaac and his seed. He took the penalty in the role of the Melchizedek priesthood, while fulfilling all the Levitical requirements. He brought the two together, merging the Abrahamic covenant and the Melchizedek priesthood together and when He did that, He confirmed the covenant. That means He set a seal on it so no one can disannul it. Herein God said, "I have sealed the Abrahamic covenant with a Melchizedek offering."

The Lord has made known six things essential in preaching His Word. Preaching should reveal the **person** of God, the **presence** of God, the **promises** of God, the **provision** of God, the **plan** of God and the **purpose** of God. The Abrahamic covenant and the truth of the Melchizedek priesthood reveal all six of these things.

MELCHISEDEK – THE PATRIARCH SHEM

"As we have seen, foreign and especially Hebrew words, were introduced into the Egyptian inscriptions, and it seems probable that "Philition" was equivalent to the Hebrew word Melchisedek – which has a similar meaning – "King of Righteousness," for the priests seem to have known, like the Jews who compiled the Targum, that Melchisedek was Shem.

"The identification of Melchisedek with Shem naturally seems incredible to people who find it difficult to believe in the great age ascribed to Shem in the Bible, namely six hundred years, for since he is said to have been one hundred years old at the time of the deluge (about 2348 B.C.) he must have been nearly five hundred at the time that Melchisedek met Abraham (Gen. xiv), whose date is given as 1996-1821 B.C. (*Cambridge History,* Vol. I, p. 166)."

"In Jerusalem, however, no doubt can have been felt as to the great age of Shem, for 'the Jews, in admitting this official or personal superiority of Melchisedek to Abraham, sought to account for it by alleging that the royal priest was no other than Shem, the most pious of Noah's sons' (Kitto's *Cyclopedia of Biblical Literature*, Vol. III, p. 125).

"M. Lenormant writes. 'The commonly received opinion among the Jews, according to Jerome, and also among the Samaritans, was that Melchisedek was the patriarch Shem' (*Ancient History of the East,* p. 83).

From. *The Man Who Built the Great Pyramid, by* Mrs. Sydney Bristowe, p. 137

The Office of Melchizedek
Chapter Two

The first recorded account of the existence of Melchizedek begins with Genesis 14. His role began before the time of that account and extends throughout the Scriptures. Shem not only lived more years than Abraham, but was born before Abraham and outlived Abraham. Abraham's grandson Jacob was 50 years old when Shem died. It is very possible and highly likely that Jacob conversed with Shem. Another profound truth is that when Abraham met Shem in Genesis 14, the book of Hebrews tells us Abraham's great grandson, Levi, paid tithe while he was still in the loins of his great grandfather. This incident took place 172 years before Levi was born, yet this tithe was paid to Melchizedek. So if Levi paid tithe the whole priesthood tribe also paid tithe through him.

The chart in the appendix illustrates that Shem was the third generation from Adam **by word of mouth.** Adam lived 930 years. Following this timeline, Adam was still living 243 years after Methuselah was born. Lamech, who was Noah's father, lived 56 years during the life of Adam. Adam was the first man of his genealogy or race. Lamech was the ninth generation following Adam. He had been born during Adam's lifetime and was still living when Adam died. It is very possible that Adam, having firsthand knowledge of what took place in the Garden, passed that knowledge down his family line, all the way to Lamech, and thence to Noah the father of Shem. Lamech lived 93 years after the birth of Shem. Methuselah, who lived the longest of any man in the Bible, lived 98 years after Shem was born. Lamech means the 'avenger or destroyer." The name Methuselah means; 'When the flood comes he shall die." Or turn it around and say, "When he dies the flood shall come." He died the same year that the flood came. If Methuselah and Lamech talked to Adam, it is highly probable that Methuselah and Lamech also talked to Shem. Since Shem, by word of mouth, is only the third generation from Adam, he and his descendants possessed knowledge and birthright blessings preserving their family heritage.

Everything that God has done and is doing He has based it upon His covenant relationship and oaths. Basically, whenever a covenant is made between God and man, whether it be Abraham or someone else, God initiates that covenant and then swears that He is going to fulfill that covenant He made. For example, God blessed Abraham and made a covenant with him which gave Abraham the right to pass that covenantal blessing to his son. That covenant then gave Isaac the right to pass the covenantal blessing to his son and on down the line.

The institutions of the Old Testament that were highly respected in the Adamic race were: *1) Fatherhood.* The oldest living patriarch of the Adamic race at any given time was considered to be the king or civil authority of that race. *2) Priesthood.* The oldest living patriarch was considered to be the religious authority of that race. This authority was totally different than what we live under today, because authority today is being despised by present society. We live in an age of rebellion against parental, civil, business and religious authority. We are in an age where we no longer respect fatherhood or priesthood. The foundations of an orderly society are being destroyed: fatherhood, priesthood and civil authority, all of which are derived directly from the Scriptures. They all have one source. They all derive their power and origin from God. So our society lives in rebellion against authority and ultimately against God.

THE OATH AND THE SEAL

In the Scriptures we see some of the genealogical connections between Shem and the other men in the Bible living before and after him. In the concordances the name Melchisedek means *royal, king of right or rightful king or altogether just.* In everything that God has done, He has done by oath. Every major relationship that He set up and established, He established *by oath.* An oath is "a declaration that one will speak the truth, keep a promise and remain faithful to that promise." The Biblical definition of an oath is *"to be complete."* The method to ensure completion is to declare something seven times. It is as though you swear to something seven times, symbolizing completion. If the contractor swears an oath seven times, that makes it a binding legal document and no one can change it. So God swears and He cannot change the statement; *"Thou art a priest forever."* He made a covenant with Abraham, Isaac and Jacob, and He cannot repent.

One of the reasons for blood sacrifice is to show the death of the two parties involved. Even though the sacrifice was an animal, that blood had to be sacrificed, which represented the two parties who were involved in that oath. Party A and Party B made the agreement, but the third party had to die. God was not going to kill Isaac, so a ram had to die as a third party. It represented the fact that these two parties cannot change their minds. Dead men cannot change their minds. That is one of the meanings of the blood sacrifice in the Old Testament. When Jesus died on the cross He sealed the New Covenant with the House of Israel and the House of Judah, represented by His shed blood. He cannot change His mind. When some theologians tell us just the opposite, "when Jesus died He did away with election of the House of Israel and the House of Judah," they are mistaken. He sealed this contract with His blood. He cannot change His mind. His death was not a sacrifice of an animal as prescribed in the Old Testament. He was the incarnate Son of God; God in flesh who gave His own life. So what He is saying is, "I will give My life, I will sacrifice My flesh and My blood and will seal this covenant forever" (Jeremiah 31:31-34).

The Melchizedek calling and principle was and is within the Adamic race. Starting at Genesis 1:26 it says, *"And God said let us make man in our image, after our likeness and let them have dominion over the fish of the sea, over the fowl of the air and over the cattle and over all the earth and over every creeping thing that creepeth upon the earth. So God created man in His own image, in the image of God created He him, male and female created He them and God blessed them."* There was a statement by God which constituted an oath. Adam is going to have dominion. *"And God said,"* are the first three words in verse 26. The first four words in verse 28 are a blessing. *"And God blessed them."* This is a Melchizedek type principle. **He swears and then He blesses.** God blessed them and God said unto them, "be fruitful, multiply, replenish and subdue, have dominion." That is an oath. That is a Melchizedek type oath over the fowl of the air, fish of the sea and every living thing that moves upon the earth.

Adam was given dominion. First came the oath, second the blessing, the Melchizedek type blessing and principle that had begun before Genesis 14.

Another thing about **Adam** as related in Genesis four is that he taught his sons, Cain and Abel, to make sacrifices as priests. This was long before the Law of Moses. Genesis 4:3: *"And in process of time it came to pass that Cain brought of the fruit of the ground an offering unto the Lord. And Abel also brought of the firstlings of his flock and fat thereof. And the Lord had respect unto Abel and to his offering."* Where did they get this idea of bringing a sacrifice. They got it from Adam. Adam had to get it from the Almighty Himself. So we see this in Adam. **dominion and priesthood.**

THE ALTAR

Noah functioned as a priest and *"builded an altar unto the Lord"* (Gen. 8:20). Where did he get the idea to build an altar. This was several generations later after Adam. He got it from his father Lamech, who got it from Methuselah, who got it from Adam. This priestly calling was Adam's calling and dominion. He passed that dominion blessing down to his family. Adam passed that down to Seth and Seth passed it down to Enos and to Canaan. He passed it to Mahalaleel and Jared and Enoch gave it to Methuselah. This was a Godly line. Noah built an ark, and after this flood was over he pronounced a blessing upon one of his sons and a curse upon one grandson. In Genesis 9:25 it says, *"Cursed be Canaan."* That curse took a real affect. These were not idle words. He said, "Canaan, you are going to be a servant of servants unto your brethren." In verse

26 he said, *"Blessed be the Lord God of Shem and Canaan shall be his servant."* Then concerning Japheth, *"God shall enlarge Japheth, he shall dwell in the tents of Shem and Canaan shall be his servant."*

Where did Noah get the authority to utter such a curse and a blessing. He got it from the patriarchal authority that extended all the way back to Adam. When Melchizedek blessed Abraham, 172 years before Levi was born, it mentions Levi only as being in the loins of Abraham. Levi had eleven brothers who were also in the loins of Abraham. There is nothing mentioned in Genesis 14 about Levi. So when the blessing was uttered upon Abram it was conferred upon all of his offspring as well. The writer of Hebrews only mentions the fact that Levi, being the priestly tribe, paid tithe unto this greater priesthood. What about all the other sons. What about grandsons Ephraim and Manasseh? Of course, they were also in the loins of Abraham so they got a Melchizedek blessing as well. So this royal and priestly family of Abraham was blessed by a royal priestly order called Melchizedek.

Later on, Christ fulfilled this Melchizedek order, which was a role and purpose given by oath out of the mouth of God, starting in Genesis chapter one. This principle of oath was passed down by patriarchal authority and Shem held it at the time of Genesis 14. When God made the oath through the mouth of Melchizedek, He cannot repent or change His mind. Melchizedek had the authority as a king/priest to put a kingly blessing in Abraham so Judah and Levi could come forth later on, bearing those blessings: the one bearing the kingship and the other the priestly office. Then Moses made the statement in Exodus, "I will make you kings and priests." Where did Moses get that authority. Did he just pull that out of the air? No, he got that from the patriarchal authority already conferred on him.

Now was Moses the Melchizedek of his day? That's possible. Adam fulfilled the Melchizedek order of his day. Adam passed it to Seth and Seth passed it down the line to the next recipient and then passed to the next recipient, etc. The Melchizedek order didn't start with Shem. It was just the highlight of the Melchizedek order in Genesis 14.

Abraham functioned as a priest as we find in Genesis 12:8. *"And he removed from thence unto a mountain on the east of Bethel, and pitched his tent, having Bethel on the west and Hai on the east: and there he built an altar unto the LORD, and called upon the name of the LORD."* Abraham was following a patriarchal order of **building an altar**. In Genesis 13:4 it says: *"Unto the place of the altar, which he had made there at the first: and there Abram called on the name of the LORD."* Verse 18: *"Then Abram removed his tent, and came and dwelt in the plain of Mamre, which is in Hebron, and built there an altar unto the LORD."* Everywhere he went he took his altar with him and functioned as a priest long before the Levitical order ever came into existence. In Genesis 22:9 is described the altar. *"And they came to the place which God had told him of; and Abraham built an altar there, and laid the wood in order, and bound Isaac his son, and laid him on the altar upon the wood."* Where did Abraham get this idea. He received it from his forefathers. In Genesis 22:2 God speaks to Abraham and chooses his son. Abraham already had another son, but it is as though that other son did not exist when it came to the covenant and the birthright. God made this oath, *"in Isaac shall thy seed be called."*

That is an oath from the Almighty God. The Spirit takes those words and places them deep into our understanding and lets us know that God made an unalterable oath when He swore unto Abraham. He already swore unto Abraham concerning a covenant and then He says, "I have to perpetuate this covenant. I am going to perpetuate it in his natural son Isaac." That is the oath of God and He cannot change it. We must believe in the sovereignty and verity of God. **Verity** is immutable truthfulness. So Isaac is chosen by oath. Then God further declares an oath concerning Isaac. In Genesis 22:15-18: *"And the angel of the LORD called unto Abraham out of heaven the second time, And said, By myself have I sworn,* [God's oath, as though he had said it seven times] *saith the LORD, for because thou hast done this thing, and hast not withheld thy son, thine only son:* [He had another son, but God said **thine only son.** *That in blessing I will bless thee, and in multiplying I* will [not 'might'] *multiply thy seed as the stars of the heaven, and as the sand which is upon the sea shore; and thy seed shall possess the gate of his enemies; And in thy seed shall all the nations of the earth be blessed; because thou hast obeyed my voice."*

Genesis 25:5 says: *"And Abraham gave all that he had unto Isaac."* Here, God is speaking to Isaac in Genesis 26:3: *"Sojourn in this land, and I will be with thee, and will bless thee; for unto thee, and unto thy seed, I will give all these countries, and I will perform the oath which I sware unto Abraham thy father;"* God said, 'I will perform the oath.' How did any one of these men, Adam, Noah, Abraham, or Isaac receive their blessing. By the oath of God Himself. By His spoken Word, uttered in their hearing.

Isaac blessed Jacob as recorded in Genesis 25. Jacob receives the birthright. We read the story of how he deceived his father and in spite of the deception he received the birthright and God sanctioned it. God Himself said, *"Jacob have I loved and Esau have I hated."* Let God be God in His sovereignty. So Jacob has been given the birthright blessing although to us that would seem unfair.

Genesis 27:28-29: *"Therefore God give thee of the dew of heaven, and the fatness of the earth, and plenty of corn and wine: Let people serve thee, and nations bow down to thee: be lord over thy brethren, and let thy mother's sons bow down to thee: cursed be every one that curseth thee, and blessed be he that blesseth thee."* Jacob received the birthright and a blessing. Esau received a blessing, but it was not the birthright blessing. There is a difference between a blessing and a birthright blessing because the Scripture says, *"and Abram gave all that he had unto his son,"* Isaac. These material possessions were signs of his blessing that he was passing down through his patriarchal authority, not to Ishmael but to Isaac. Isaac had the birthright and now Jacob has the birthright.

Jacob built an altar as shown in Genesis 33:20. *"And he erected there an altar, and called it Elelohe Israel."* Where did he get this idea. He received it from his father Isaac. In Genesis *35:1:* *"And God said unto Jacob, Arise, go up to Bethel, and dwell there: and make there an altar unto God, that appeared unto thee when thou fleddest from the face of Esau thy brother. Then Jacob said*

unto his household, and to all that were with him, Put away the
strange gods that are among you, and be clean, and change your
garments: And let us arise, and go up to Bethel; and I will make
there an altar unto God, who answered me in the day of my distress,
and was with me in the way which I went." That made Bethel
a sacred place which the children of Israel defiled later on. In
Genesis 35:7 it says: *"And he built there an altar, and called the*
place Elbethel: because there God appeared unto him, when he
fled from the face of his brother."

The Lord says He will make *us* a kingdom of Priests. In Revelation, chapter one, He says we will be kings and priests unto our
God. We, the family of Israel, have a high calling. Where did
we get this concept of building an altar and bowing our knees
before God. We received it from our fathers and they received
it from their fathers, their fathers received it from their fathers
and so on back all the way to Adam. Abel built an altar and I am
sure Seth built an altar. Noah, Shem and Abraham built altars.
They were holy altars and they did sacrifice on them. We too
have a priestly and a kingly calling. It is in our genetic makeup
to bow and worship before the Lord God of Heaven. Altar building occurred before the Levitical order ever came into being, so
this altar was not a Levitical altar, it was a Melchizedek altar, a
royal altar. A high order of worship was unto God Himself and
passed down through this Godly line. In Genesis 32:28, we see
this about Jacob: *"And he said, Thy name shall be called no more*
Jacob, [deceiver, supplanter] *but Israel* [because he was given
royal princely authority]: *for as a prince hast thou power with*
God and with men, and hast prevailed."

That was an oath out of the mouth of God. Jacob already functioned as a priest and now the Lord is telling him there are kings in his loins. He is royalty, and is going to have civil authority in the earth. God has invested civil and religious authority in the Abrahamic family in the earth. When this God-ordained priestly and civil authority is denied, your culture will crumble. We have abdicated this calling and authority by giving it away. When you sell your birthright under the guise of political and religious correctness, you are despising the call that God has put within you. The church of today has come up with cultural and religious lies, which have weakened its spiritual and cultural effectiveness in the world. Jacob's blessing by God in changing his name was indicative of his calling to a position of authority.

THE BIRTH OF BENJAMIN

In Genesis 35:16 we read: *"And they journeyed from Bethel; and there was but a little way to come to Ephrath: and Rachel travailed, and she had hard labour. And it came to pass, when she was in hard labour, that the midwife said unto her, Fear not; thou shalt have this son also. And it came to pass, as her soul was in departing, (for she died) that she called his name Benoni* [son of my sorrow]: *but his father called him Benjamin."* Jacob took the authority to rename his son and called him Benjamin which means, 'son of my right hand." Why did Jacob do such a presumptuous thing and why did he name him Benjamin. Right hand denotes strength and blessing. Which hand did he bless Ephraim with. His right hand. This was a prophecy in naming that boy. God had already changed his name from Jacob to Israel and now he takes the authority to change his infant son's name *from sorrow to strength*. In other words, there is destiny in this child. The tribe of Benjamin was given to the House of David so that the House of David would always have spiritual light. The House of David was from whence our Lord came and the tribe of Benjamin was prophesied of in Isaiah 53 that it would stand with the Messiah, who possessed the right to rule on David's throne (Luke 1:30-33).

The Apostle Paul, the man who brought us light, was of the tribe of Benjamin. This was prophetic destiny. Jacob changed his son's name by prophetic and patriarchal authority. Where did he get this authority to bless his twelve sons. He got it from his father Isaac. A Melchizedek blessing came from the Melchizedek order. He had the authority. Not everybody had the authority to bless. It came down through this elect, preordained line. In Genesis 48:9: *"And Joseph said unto his father, They are my sons, whom God hath given me in this place. And he said, Bring them, I pray thee, unto me, and I will bless them."* This was no light thing. Jacob was saying, 'I am going to put dominion and destiny in them and their offspring.' Verse 16: *"The Angel which redeemed me from all evil, bless the lads; ..."* These are prophetic words spoken by the oath of God, because Jacob had the Melchizedek and prophetic blessing in him from his father, grandfather and all the way back to Adam. That blessing on those lads cannot be reversed and even Balaam confirmed it. (see Num. 24)

In verse 20 the record continues: *"And he blessed them that day, saying, In thee shall Israel bless, saying, God make thee as Ephraim and as Manasseh: and he set Ephraim before Manasseh."* He blessed the other sons; Reuben, Simeon, Levi, Judah, Zebulon, Issachar, Dan, Gad, Asher, Naphtali and Benjamin. Then he utters another blessing upon this dual tribe that the **Shepherd of Israel** shall be among them. We see this Melchizedek blessing given to Abraham, passed down through his son and grandson which was a dual blessing; a kingly and a priestly blessing of spiritual light and understanding. Genesis 14 was just a highlight given to us to open our understanding and to see this blessing magnified and multiplied through the descendants of Jacob.

The Melchizedek order is superior in time and rank to Levi. When Christ came, He fulfilled the Melchizedek order. He fills that office today. The Melchizedek order started with Adam, the Levitical order started with Levi. The Levitical order died, but the Melchizedek order lives on. We are living in the blessings and benefits of the Melchizedek priesthood, yet we reap the benefits of the order that ended.

In Amos 9:11 we find: *"In that day will I raise up the tabernacle of David that is fallen, and close up the breaches thereof; and I will raise up his ruins, and I will build it as in the days of old:"* The tabernacle of David was not a Levitical order. It was a Melchizedek order. In the book of Amos we read that things have crumbled and fallen apart for Israel, but Amos prophesied and said; 'now Israel (Northern House), you are going into Assyrian captivity and there will be a famine of the Word of God. Not of bread but of hearing the Word of the Lord." That was referring to two things. Basically the 400 years between Malachi and Christ could apply, but here it applied to the Assyrian captivity when the children of Israel would go into heathenism. They would become as the nations around them. They would lose their way in heathenism, idol worship, Greek philosophy, Roman mythology and all the pagan religions that they would become involved with from 745 BC all the way to the time of Christ when the Apostles and the tribe of 'light' went to them into Europe and Great Britain. So we have a minimum of 750 years of darkness.

Our own ancestors lived in darkness and heathenism. Historians tell us that the Anglo-Saxons were heathens. They were, since there was a famine of hearing the Word of God, plus the gross and grievous sins they committed. God sent Israel into captivity for this same reason. Amos records God's promise that "I am going to restore a tabernacle; not a temple, but a tabernacle." One of the characteristics of a tabernacle is that it is moveable and mobile. A temple is a permanent structure. A tabernacle can be taken down and moved when you travel. What did the children of Israel do. They traveled and migrated. Amos says, *"I will raise up the tabernacle of David that is fallen, and close up the breaches thereof; and I will raise up his ruins, and I will build it as in the days of old:."*

The Tabernacle of David is involved in the Melchizedek priesthood. The Melchizedek priesthood is the fulfillment of the restoration of the Tabernacle of David. We are surely not trying to build a Levitical temple. Anybody who goes to Palestine and thinks they are going to build a Levitical temple unto God, may build it, but it is not built unto God. It is an abomination, because the Levitical order is gone. He said He was going to build the tabernacle of David, which we are now dwelling in. David did not build a temple. David was the Melchizedek of his day and functioned both as a king and as a priest.

Through the mouth of Moses, the Lord said He would give us a calling and then He reiterates that in Revelation chapter one. "I'll make you kings and priests unto God." Sometimes this is translated as a *kingdom of priests* with dual authority. What are the two witnesses. The two witnesses of Revelation are these two callings invested in the children of Israel: civil and religious authority as both kings and priests. They are not Enoch and Elijah or Elijah and Moses or Moses and Enoch as our teachers may have told us. It is a dual calling invested in the loins of Jacob and his children. These are the two witnesses of Revelation. This world will never get to the place of civil and religious stability until Jesus Christ comes back and sits upon His throne as a priest, as stated in Zechariah chapter six. It says He is coming back and is going to sit upon a throne. Priests don't sit on thrones, but this one does, for He is the only rightful heir.

Melchizedek's Dual Office
Chapter Three

Consider the Melchizedek order as contrasted with the Levitical order. Without doubt, Shem's forefathers communed and shared a lot of God's wonderful works with Shem. Shem was the man of transition who lived both in the antediluvian and postdiluvian ages. Shem lived a total of 600 years. He lived 502 years after the flood. Imagine the volume of knowledge that he had stored up concerning the history of the world up to that point. For sure he shared it with his sons for their history could be carried down by word of mouth for many generations. It is believed that Moses wrote the five books of the Pentateuch. From the time of the incident of Shem and Abram in Genesis 14 in approximately 2000 BC, 500 years elapsed before Moses came on the scene. Vital information describing the creation was correctly carried verbally to Moses so that he could accurately write the book of Genesis. He had been given this information by word of mouth. This vital information was transmitted one to another very accurately. It was not just gossip; rather, it was transmitted down to each succeeding generation with studied accuracy because these were family and historical records. The Genesis account was conveyed with a sense of great value. All the family heirlooms of that day were held in very high esteem as well.

This Melchizedek order was passed down from generation to generation and although at times it remained in the background, it was never lost. As we study the origins of the Levitical priest-hood, more questions arise. What were the Urim and Thum-mim? How did they work? A Levitical priesthood had specific duties to perform, with particular garments and equipment prescribed for this work. The High Priest had his duties to per-form and was commanded to wear a linen ephod. Behind that garment was a pocket which contained the Urim and Thummim. The priests consulted the Urim and the Thummim for guidance until they got the answer they sought. The Levitical priesthood operated on a lower plane, but the Melchizedek priesthood oper-ated on a higher plane. The book of Hebrews uses the English word *"better,"* referring to the Melchizedek order. It was higher in rank, superior in authority and always in existence. It looked forward to the ultimate fulfillment in a Man who would be the last Melchizedek and fulfill both the Levitical priesthood and the Melchizedek priesthood.

MELCHIZEDEK - THE DUAL OFFICE

In Zechariah 6:12 this post-exilic prophet is speaking concerning restoration: *"And speak unto him, saying, 'Thus speaketh the LORD of hosts, saying, Behold the man whose name is The BRANCH; and he shall grow up out of his place, and he shall build the temple of the LORD:'* We find the root of this passage back in Isaiah 11:1: *"And there shall come forth a rod out of the stem of Jesse, and a Branch shall grow out of his roots:"* This passage teaches that the Branch is part of the root of the family of David. This One who is the Branch is an offshoot or a descendent of that Davidic tree that had been assumed dead. A tender branch, Isaiah 11 says, comes out of that tree. The Branch shall grow up out of His place. This Branch shall grow up out of His designated place, order, authority, family and foundation that He was ordained to grow up in. That place He was ordained to come out of is the family of David.

"And He shall build the temple of the Lord," [The Branch is going to build the temple of the Lord." *"Even he shall build the temple of the LORD; and he shall bear the glory, and shall sit and rule upon his throne; and he shall be a priest upon his throne: and the counsel of peace shall be between them both"* Zechariah 6:12-13. What is the temple of the Lord in the New Testament context. In the captivity the Babylonians had invaded and destroyed the city of Jerusalem and the temple. Seventy years later over 42,000 people returned to Jerusalem to rebuild the city, the walls and the temple. First it was Solomon's temple, then it was this post-exilic temple and then later Herod restored that temple which took 46 years to complete. Is that the temple the prophet Zechariah is talking about. No, there is a greater temple. The earthly Solomonic temple is on a lower plane, but Christ's temple is on a higher plane.

Jesus said in Matthew 16. *"I will build my church."* The temple that Zechariah is talking about is the church which is Christ's body. This is the temple that He is building. He is not building it as a Levitical priest. He is building it as a Melchizedek priest. Again: *"and he shall grow up out of his place, and he shall build the temple of the LORD:"* This prophet repeats himself in verse 13. *"Even he shall build the temple of the LORD; and he shall bear the glory, and shall sit and rule upon his throne;"* We can see some identification of who this root is. He came out of Jesse, David's father. He was that tender shoot or branch that came out of those roots. David was a king sitting on a throne and this Branch is going to sit on a throne. *"and he shall be a priest upon his throne:"* Priests don't sit on thrones, but this One does. He is a King/Priest, bearing the dual office. *"and he shall be a priest upon his throne: and the counsel of peace shall be between them both."* Who is the 'both'? These two offices, King and Priest. No more opposition against one another or competition between them can occur because one man is going to fulfill both offices. He did not discard the throne when He took on the office of priest. He did not discard his priestly garments when He sat on His throne. So we have a priest sitting upon His throne and this one can be none other than Jesus Christ Himself. Revelation 1:5: *"And from Jesus Christ, who is the faithful witness, and the first begotten of the dead, and the prince of the kings of the earth. Unto him that loved us,* [as a faithful witness] *and washed us* [as a priest] *from our sins in his own blood, And hath made us kings and priests unto God and his Father; to him be glory and dominion for ever and ever. Amen.*

Three offices are described here, **Prophet, Priest** and **King**. As **prophet,** He is designated first by John as the faithful witness. Second, He is the first-begotten from the dead. Instead of an animal sacrifice He gave Himself and then came out of the grave, therefore He is the first-begotten of the dead. As a **priest** He washed us from our sins in His own blood. Third, as the **prince of the kings** of the earth, He hath made us kings and priests unto God and His Father.

He loved us, He washed us and He is making us. We are not a finished product, for He is making us kings and priests. Some have translated this as 'a kingdom of priests' which is accurate. Is He making us Levitical priests or Melchizedek priests?

Zechariah said He is going to hold two offices, king and priest. He has a company of people that He is making. He speaks to them and He loves them as a faithful witness. That is the foundation of God's relationship to man. Then He washed us and continues to wash us, I John 1:9. If we sin, He is faithful and just to forgive us. He will continually forgive us for our sins and continually cleanse us from all unrighteousness. When we get saved we are covered by the blood of Christ and are thereby in the process of being saved which is continual, like a baby being born and growing up. How long does it take for a baby to be born. He is not mature at birth. He is totally dependent upon someone else. A baby can't talk and has no education, but the child is in the process of learning. That is the way we are in the Christian life. We are birthed into this new life in Christ, this regeneration, and then this new life continues as a process of living. He loved us and He is **loving** us, He washed us and He is **washing** us. He made us and He is **making** us. It will take time to make us into a pleasing vessel, but He is doing this in the dual office as a Melchizedek priest.

Revelation 1:11 says: *"Saying, I am Alpha and Omega, the first and the last:"* That is not a Levitical priest speaking, but a Melchizedek priest. Verse 12 adds: *"And I turned to see the voice that spake with me. And being turned, I saw seven golden candlesticks;"* Verse 20: *"The mystery of the seven stars which thou sawest in my right hand, and the seven golden candlesticks. The seven stars are the angels of the seven churches: and the seven candlesticks which thou sawest are the seven churches."* Those seven churches were part of His Church, which is His Body, He said He was going to build.

Who is this, who holds these seven candlesticks. See verse 13-18: *"And in the midst of the seven candlesticks one like unto the Son of man, clothed with a garment down to the foot, and girt about the paps with a golden girdle. His head and his hairs were white like wool, as white as snow; and his eyes were as a flame of fire. And his feet like unto fine brass, as if they burned in a furnace; and his voice as the sound of many waters.* [That describes more than a Levitical Priest."] *And he had in his right hand seven stars: and out of his mouth went a sharp two-edged sword:* [The sword was not part of the Levitical priest's garments.] *and his countenance was as the sun shineth in his strength. And when I saw him, I fell at his feet as dead. And he laid his right hand upon me, saying unto me, Fear not; I am the first and the last: I am he that liveth, and was dead; and, behold, I am alive for evermore, Amen; and have the keys of hell and of death."* **Death may be the king of terrors, but Jesus is the King of kings.**

THE EARTHLY MINISTRY OF JESUS

In the earthly ministry of our Lord, Jesus functioned both as a Levitical priest and a Melchizedek priest. Jesus Christ was God in the flesh. *"And the Word became flesh."* He is not God number two. He is not the second person of the Godhead. John **did not** say in John 1:14 "The Word became **two**." He said the Word became flesh. One writer said He took upon Himself the form of Abraham. What for. So He might communicate with Abraham and his children. **Jesus is God.** We need to take Him out of the human class and put Him in the God class. Jesus Christ had two natures, but one will. He was 100% man and 100% God. He prayed in the garden, 'not My will, but Thine be done.' His will was one with His Father. In the days of His flesh, Jesus, from a child, was raised and lived in the Levitical order. Therefore it was imperative that He fulfill Old Covenant requirements.

In Luke 2:21 it tells us: *"And when eight days was accomplished for the circumcising of the child."* Jesus as an eight day old baby was circumcised according to the Law of Moses and this was carried out by the Levitical priesthood (Lev. 12:1,40). So at eight days old Jesus' parents presented Him to a Levitical priest and to that order. Luke 2:22: *"And when the days of her purification according to the law of Moses were accomplished, they brought him to Jerusalem, to present him to the Lord;"* His mother Mary was purified according to the Law of Moses (Leviticus 12:8; Exodus 13: 22, 34; Numbers 3, 18). Jesus was fulfilling the Law of Moses and the Levitical order.

Luke 1:27 says, *"and when the parents brought in the child Jesus, to do for him after the custom of the law,"* they were showing their subjection unto the Law of Moses. During His earthly ministry and life, Jesus attended Passover feasts. *"Now his parents went to Jerusalem every year at the feast of the Passover"* Luke 2:41. It says **every** year. Every year at the Feast of the Passover His parents followed the Levitical order and Jesus went with them while living at home, under their order and dominion. *"And when he was twelve years old, they went up to Jerusalem after the custom of the feast"* (Luke 2:42). Since He went at twelve years old, no doubt He went at one year old, at two and all the other years as well. He respected the Law of God as given to Moses. In the book of John we see where Jesus attended a Passover Feast when he was 30 ½ years old. In John 2:13 it reads, *"And the Jews' passover was at hand, and Jesus went up to Jerusalem."*

It started in the Old Testament as the LORD's Passover, but by this time it had become the Jews' Passover. In John chapter 5, He is 31 ½ years old. In John 6:34 Jesus was 32 ½ years old and at 33 years old, just six months later, He went to a Tabernacle meeting. At 33 ½ years old in John 11:55, *"And the Jews' passover was nigh at hand: and many went out of the country up to Jerusalem before the passover, to purify themselves."* So throughout His earthly ministry He went to a Passover celebration every year. We see where our Lord ate a prepared Passover meal in Matthew 26:17: *"Now the first day of the feast of unleavened bread the disciples came to Jesus, saying unto him, Where wilt thou that we prepare for thee to eat the passover?"* They actually prepared a meal.

So, did Jesus despise the Levitical order. No, He came to fulfill it. In John 7 at that Tabernacle meeting when He was 33 years old, six months before His death, He attended this feast and on the last day, Jesus stood up an. said, *"If any man thirst let him come unto me and drink.* (John 7:37). He was fulfilling the Levitical order and its command to go to the feast, but when He opened His mouth He was in the realm of the Melchizedek order and not the Levitical order. When He opened His mouth, He said: *"If any man thirst, let him come unto me, and drink. He that believeth on me, as the scripture hath said, out of his belly shall flow rivers of living water."* Levi could not offer that. Aaron could not offer that nor could any other earthly priest. Jesus stepped out of the Levitical Priesthood into the Melchizedek priesthood at that moment. In His flesh He was obeying the Levitical order, but out of His spirit He was functioning in the Melchizedek order. He didn't say bring a sacrifice, a lamb or turtle dove if you are poor. This was an offer and a prophecy because He said, in verse 39: *"(But this spake he of the Spirit, which they that believe on him should receive: for the Holy Ghost was not yet given; because that Jesus was not yet glorified.)"* Glorified? His crucifixion in the flesh was part of His glorification in the Spirit.

We have to view this idea from two perspectives. Jesus, while fulfilling the Levitical order submitted to circumcision at eight days old. He was presented to the Lord. His mother was purified after 40 days according to the Law of Moses. He did everything according to the custom of the Law. He attended the Passover Feasts and the Tabernacle Feasts. It was here He spoke of the Holy Ghost, because the Holy Ghost was not yet given. His sacrifice had not yet been offered and His total pre-eminence had not yet been fulfilled. In His flesh, respecting and obeying the order of Levi, Jesus suffered and died.

Jesus was chosen on the tenth day of the month Abib, just as the sacrifice in Egypt was chosen on the tenth day of that month (Exodus 12:3). They set aside that spotless lamb on the tenth day of the month Abib, which was the first month of the sacred calendar of the Hebrews. His triumphal entry into Jerusalem occurred on that same day. When the people strewed their clothes in the way and waved palm leaves saying, 'Hosanna in *the Highest*, this is He,' (Matt. 21) they called Him the son of David. They were following the order of choosing the sacrifice. Jesus was that spotless sacrificial lamb, holy, and without sin. Jesus died on the fourteenth day of Abib, the day of preparation (Exodus 12), fulfilling the Law even in His death. Jesus was crucified at nine o'clock in the morning, the time of the morning oblation according to the Old Testament. The Hebrews had two offerings daily, one in the morning at 9 a.m. and the other in the evening at 3 p.m. Jesus was hung on the cross at nine o'clock and stayed on the cross for six hours and died at three o'clock in the afternoon. That would give time for them to take His body off the cross and bury it in a sepulcher nearby, before the coming of the Sabbath. Thus He fulfilled the Levitical order in His life and in His death.

Now from the sixth hour there was darkness over all the land unto the ninth hour. That sixth hour of the morning was twelve noon. From noon to three p.m., which was three hours, there was darkness over the earth. Something happened as recorded in Luke 23:45 when He died as a Levitical priest. Being hung on the cross at nine a.m., staying there until noon, then darkness came and remained there until three p.m., which would be six hours on the cross, until the ninth hour. At noon, the sun was darkened and the veil in the temple was rent (torn) from the top to the bottom. That did not happen during the Old Testament sacrifices. Something out of the ordinary had happened. Melchizedek was now stepping forward. This man died fulfilling the Levitical Law. When He died, this veil which was six inches thick made of interwoven material which could not be broken, tore apart from the top to the bottom. It split from the top, which was far above the reach of any individual, exposing the farce that remained behind that veil. No Ark of the Covenant, Mercy Seat, Cherubim with their wings outspread and no Glory cloud were there. It took Melchizedek to expose that system that had held the people in bondage for so long. Levi couldn't do it, but Melchizedek did!

The veil of the temple and the temple itself were everything to the people. They were the center of Israelite culture. The holy of holies was the thing that had made that temple holy and sacred and now its emptiness had been exposed. Nothing was there. The Ark was gone. The Holy of Holies was empty and being that it was nothing, the temple itself was nothing. When Jesus said, *"If any man thirst,"* He did not say go to the temple or go to Levi, He said, **"Come unto me."** Levi is now fading into the distance and Melchizedek is stepping forward. Did He despise the Law. No, He rather fulfilled the Law. We are speaking about just the sacrificial law. He fulfilled it to the letter. Then He said we need something better. Much better. That is when He stepped forward and said, "Come unto Me." When He died on the cross, He died fulfilling the Levitical order, but the ministry of Melchizedek lived on. Did any of the sacrifices in the Old Testament come back to life, whether it be a little turtle dove, a lamb or a goat. Of course not. But this sacrifice came back to life. He died as a Levitical priest, but He resurrected as a Melchizedek priest. Endless life was His and that is why He told John in Revelation 1: *"I was dead. I am the first and the last."* He can't be first and last as a Levitical priest. **He was first and last as a Melchizedek priest.**

Jesus was buried before the high Sabbath began because Deuteronomy says that no dead body shall remain on the tree overnight. So they had to fulfill the law and get Him down off the tree. By fulfilling the Levitical order, it proved His humanity. We don't believe in deicide, our God was 100% man and 100% God. When they crucified our Lord, He died as a man. He was man's perfect sacrifice to God. He was God's perfect Man and man's perfect God. He died fulfilling the Levitical order and proving His humanity.

What about His immaculate conception in Matthew 1:18? The angel Gabriel told His mother Mary, **"*That which is born of thee is of the Holy Ghost.*"** This is not a Levitical priest. This has to be somebody greater than that. Then the angel appeared to Joseph with a surprising announcement: *"While he thought on these things, an angel of the Lord appeared unto Joseph in a dream saying, Joseph, thou son of David, fear not to take unto thee Mary thy wife, for that which is conceived of her is of the Holy Ghost."* The Lord Himself names His son, as Jacob named his youngest boy. Rachel may have called him the son of her weakness, sorrow and infirmity, but the father called him, the son of his strength or his right hand. Joseph and Mary were not given a choice as to the name of their baby. The Father named Him.

What about Gabriel's annunciation to Mary. It tells us: *"Fear not Mary, for thou hast found favor with God and thou shalt conceive in thy womb and bring forth a son and shall call His name Jesus."* Mary did not have a choice in the matter. *"He shall be great, He shall be called the Son of the highest and the Lord God shall give unto Him **the** throne....* (Luke 1:31-32). It is the same throne that David had. He's the Branch, the offshoot of the family tree of Jesse and He shall reign over the house of Jacob forever and of His kingdom there shall be no end. He is going to reign, not as a Levite, but as a Melchizedek king/priest. Zacharias, father of John the Baptist, also prophesied, saying: *"Blessed be the Lord God of Israel for He has visited and redeemed His people, and hath raised up a horn of salvation for us in the house of his servant David"* (Luke 1:68-69).

What about the prophecy of Simeon. *"Behold there was a man in Jerusalem whose name was Simeon, and the same man was just and devout, waiting for the consolation of Israel and the Holy Ghost was upon Him, And it was revealed to him by the Holy Ghost that he should not see death before he had seen the Lord's Christ. And he came by the Spirit into the temple, and when the parents brought in the child Jesus to do for him after the custom of the law, then he took he him up in his arms and* blessed *God and said,"* [keep that in mind, he blessed God first and said,] *"Lord now lettest thy servant depart in peace according to thy word, for mine eyes have seen thy salvation."* Simeon was holding the Salvation of God in his hands and he knew it.

John the Baptist gave testimony not to a Levitical priest but to a Melchizedek priest when he said, *"Behold the lamb of God."* John had two disciples behind him and he said, "There goes the Lamb of God which takes away the sin of the world." How is He going to do that. He is going to fulfill one order and bring it to a close and then He is going to execute another, a better and a higher order from heaven. Then came another sign with the voice from heaven at His water baptism. What was the message of the voice. On the surface, this was just a natural act of one man dipping another man into water, but all of a sudden the Melchizedek announcement came out of the heavens: *"This is my beloved son in whom I am well pleased."*

What tribe was Moses from. He was a Levite. *" The Lord spake unto Moses saying, speak unto Aaron and unto his sons saying on this wise, ye shall bless the children of Israel, saying unto them. The LORD bless thee and keep thee, the Lord make His face shine upon thee and be gracious unto thee. The Lord lift up His countenance upon thee and give thee peace. And they shall put my name on the children of Israel and I will bless them"* (Numbers 6:22-27). That is the Mosaic or Aaronic blessing, which is also known as the Levitical Priesthood blessing. But the Scripture records a higher blessing. It took place before Numbers chapter six, when Noah looked at his son Shem and said; *"blessed be the LORD God of Shem."* The Levitical order operates in the natural *to bless the people of God.* The Melchizedek order *blesses the God of the people.* Levi blessed the people, asking God to *"make His face to shine upon thee, be gracious, the Lord lift up His countenance, the LORD give thee peace."* But the Melchizedek blessing is to bless the God of the people first. Blessed be the LORD God of Shem. Levitical blessing is looking **downward** to the **people of God**. The Melchizedek blessing is looking **upward** to the **God of the people**. That is the difference between the two blessings.

In Genesis 14 we also find an example of this Melchizedek blessing that we have referred to before. *"Melchizedek king of Salem brought forth bread and wine and he was the priest of the most high God and he blessed him and said, blessed be Abram of the most high God, possessor of heaven and earth and blessed be the most high God which hath delivered thine enemies into thy hand."* What was the Melchizedek blessing in the book of Luke. Simeon was holding this baby in his hands and said that it had been revealed to him by the Holy Ghost that he would not see death until he had seen the promised Messiah. He came into the temple by the Spirit and picked up the baby. Luke records *"then took he him up in his arms and he blessed God."* Holding the baby he blessed God. That is the Melchizedek blessing here. When you meet somebody or you greet your brother or sister in Christ, you can give them a Levitical blessing and say 'Bless you brother' or you can give them a Melchizedek blessing and say 'Bless the Lord.' That blessing is not only to God, but to your brother and sister also. In other words, nothing is wrong with the Levitical blessing, but there is a higher blessing.

This Melchizedek blessing is conferred on the recipient *only by oath.* Was Simeon the Melchizedek of his day when he conferred this blessing upon this eight day old baby. This same Melchizedek blessing was the one that Noah conferred upon Shem and Shem conferred upon Abraham and now Simeon upon Jesus. It was conferred upon the earthly Jesus. I am comfortable with the fact that Simeon was holding that office as a natural man and he conferred it upon the Lord Jesus in the natural and then Jesus functioned in that office. That is how He could function legally according to the law of the Melchizedek order in His earthly ministry. The presence of the Melchizedek "office" hovered over the people of God from the outset, taking up "residence" in man from Shem to Christ.

Melchizedek Authority
Chapter Four

In both Old and New Testaments, we observe men living their natural lives and suddenly God takes over and changes them completely. The Apostle Paul was operating in the box that he was trained in; the strict dimensions of Phariseeism and Talmudism. As he traveled enroute to Damascus, suddenly there shone a light from heaven that changed his life. Paul's whole mentality and way of life was drastically and suddenly changed from a Levitical paradigm of religious legalism to a Melchisedek experience in Jesus Christ. Before his conversion Paul was restricted to his traditional religious box. We may also restrict God unintentionally. Let us allow God to burst open our boxes and break our constricting paradigm, whatever it might be. Let us wade out into the deep, let it come up to our ankles, to our shins, our waist and let us wade out into a new place. We are talking about the Kingdom of God, not a new denomination or a new church structure. We are talking about the order of Melchizedek that is now in place and that we now have the privilege to enter. We restrict ourselves by saying, 'I'm not used to that' or 'that is not the way I understand it' or 'that is not the way I have operated all of my life;' or 'don't bother me with any new ideas.' The Melchizedek order is far greater than our religious order.

If we are not careful, we may have a tendency to slip back into the Levitical order, little by little. I believe in the Law of God. Part of our problem in the world today is, we disdain or ignore the Law of God. Four categories of the Law exist, the Law of **Ordinances**, Commandments, Statutes and Judgments. When the priesthood changed, only one fourth of the Law was changed, which was composed of the Ordinances. When it was changed it was drastically changed. In the Old Testament an imperfect priesthood was followed by an imperfect atonement and imperfect sacrifices, which had to be repeated every year on the Day of Atonement.

Examining the Levitical order, Leviticus 9:1-3 says: "*And it came to pass on the eighth day, that Moses called Aaron and his sons, and the elders of Israel; And he said unto Aaron, Take thee a young calf for a sin offering, and a ram for a burnt offering, without blemish, and offer them before the LORD. And unto the children of Israel thou shalt speak, saying, Take ye a kid of the goats for a sin offering; and a calf and a lamb, both of the first year, without blemish, for a burnt offering;.* Verses 1 and 2 are concerned with a sin offering for Aaron and his sons. Verse 3 and following describes a sin offering for all the people. Verse 7 says: "*And Moses said unto Aaron, Go unto the altar, and offer thy sin offering,* [Aaron's own sin offering] *and thy burnt offering, and make an atonement for thyself,* [for Aaron, an imperfect priest] *and for the people: and offer the offering of the people, and make an atonement for them; as the LORD commanded.*"

Aaron, the man who is standing in the gap between God and Israel, first needs an offering for himself. What kind of a representative is he. He is a God-appointed representative, but he is imperfect. Verse 8 says: "*Aaron therefore went unto the altar, and slew the calf of the sin offering, which was for himself.*" Aaron, the High Priest, had to make atonement first for himself before he could make atonement for the people. We thus have an imperfect system in place in the Old Testament and Paul tells us that it fell short, because of its weakness.

Leviticus 16:11-13 says: *"And Aaron shall bring the bullock of the sin offering, which is for himself, and shall make an atonement for himself, and for his house, and shall kill the bullock of the sin offering which is for himself: And he shall take a censer full of burning coals of fire from off the altar before the LORD, and his hands full of sweet incense beaten small, and bring it within the vail: And he shall put the incense upon the fire before the LORD, that the cloud of the incense may cover the mercy seat that is upon the testimony, that he die not:.* In other words, he needed to be covered with blood. An atonement of blood was needed to be made for Aaron, otherwise if he entered unworthily into the Most Holy Place his life would be taken. The purpose for this sacrifice was 'that he die not.' Herein we see the great weakness of the Levitical Order. DEATH. That is the greatest weakness. What is the greatest strength of the Melchizedek Order. LIFE. Life is the biggest difference, the strongest, most powerful and most impacting difference that exists between the two orders.

Leviticus 16:6 says: *"And Aaron shall offer his bullock of the sin offering, which is for himself, and make an atonement for himself, and for his house."* That passage alone is enough evidence to show us the weakness and carnality of the Levitical Order of priests. They were just men. They were chosen men and did not bring this calling unto themselves, but were nevertheless carnal. The whole tribe had been set apart to do priestly work and were called of God to do this work for the whole house of Israel. But where is Aaron today. He is in his grave. Where are his sons. They, too, are in their graves, as are all their succeeding generations. They were all overcome by the greatest enemy of all men, which is death. They could do everything commanded by God. They could make all the offerings, go through all the routines and consecrations that they were required to do, but when it came down to meeting the final enemy; the enemy won. Death was inherent in their bodies, but in the Melchizedek Order there is no death. This Order is LIFE!

THE CONTRAST

A total of fourteen different contrasts between the Orders of Melchizedek and Levi are listed in the seventh chapter of Hebrews. The Order of Levi paid tithes, while the Order of Melchizedek received them. In verse 9: *"And as I may so say, Levi also, who receiveth tithes, payed tithes in Abraham."* He received tithes from the people in his physical body later on, but in the loins of Abraham before Levi was ever born he paid tithes to the greater priesthood of Melchizedek. Verse 4: *"Now consider how great this man was, unto whom even the patriarch Abraham gave the tenth of the spoils."*

The Melchizedek Priesthood was not conferred by descent. The Order of Levi was inherited; it was held by descent. In vers. 5: *"And verily they that are of the sons of Levi, who receive the office of the priesthood, have a commandment to take tithes of the people according to the law, that is, of their brethren, though they* [all] *come out of the loins of Abraham:.* The Levitical Order was descended from only one tribe. If you were not born of the tribe of Levi you could not function as a priest. Yet the Melchizedek Priesthood, the greater one residing in Jesus Christ Himself, did not come out of the tribe of Levi, but out of the tribe of Judah. Verse 14: *"For it is evident that our Lord sprang out of Juda; of which tribe Moses spake nothing concerning priesthood."* God made a priesthood order from Levi, but the greatest priest, Jesus Christ Himself, He chose to bring from another tribe. Did God go against His own order, law and nature. Of course not. God can do whatever He wants to do whenever He chooses. **Let God be God in His sovereignty and omniscience.**

PETER AND JOHN

In the Old Testament, Levi was the priest. Jesus chose eleven disciples (we won't count Judas) to be closest to Him and to hear His words and see His works first hand. How many of them were of the tribe of Levi? Only one. Did Jesus make a mistake? He chose men of Benjamin. I wonder if anyone ever reprimanded Jesus, saying, 'Hey, you are choosing the wrong tribe.' Benjamin was the tribe that was given to the House of David to be a light, a source of understanding, wisdom and spiritual knowledge. In Acts we read; *"Now Peter and John went up together into the temple at the hour of prayer, being the ninth hour. And a certain man lame from his mother's womb was carried, whom they laid daily at the gate of the temple which is called Beautiful, to ask alms of them that entered into the temple; Who seeing Peter and John about to go into the temple asked an alms. And Peter, fastening his eyes upon him with John, said, Look on us. And he gave heed unto them, expecting to receive something of them. Then Peter said, Silver and gold have I none; but such as I have give I thee: In the name of Jesus Christ of Nazareth rise up and walk"* (Acts 3:1-6).

Silver in the Old Testament represented **salvation** and gold represented **royalty**. So two tribes are represented here; the tribe of Levi and the tribe of Judah. What was Peter saying to this lame man, when he said, *"silver and gold have I none"*. He was putting this dual concept in natural terms which the man could understand. The man was actually asking for alms and Peter said, 'You are asking for natural alms, silver and gold, so you can .go and buy yourself some food. I have no silver, for I am not from the tribe of Levi and I have no gold, for I am not from the tribe of Judah. I have a calling greater than that of Levi and a calling greater than that of Judah. What I have, give I unto you, rise up and walk.'

Peter and John were not from the tribe of Levi, but from the tribe of Benjamin. Benjamin was closest to the heart of David, spiritually speaking. Thus, the Melchizedek Order overrode the Levitical Order. Reaction to the miracle was mixed. Some of the people rejoiced and some of them got very angry. They were the antichrist crowd and they said, 'We cannot have this. This has disturbed our usual paradigm. This takes us outside our traditional box." The lame man rose up and walked and leaped for joy in the temple which was holy, quiet and sacred. Everything was supposed to be done according to the Levitical Order and this man was running through the temple shouting, hollering and jumping. Let God be God in whatever level He wants to operate. We often restrict the Lord in our minds, and thereby lose unknown blessings. *Let God be God.* He doesn't have to restrict Himself to the tribe of Levi or to the tribe of Judah.

In Hebrews 7, the **Melchizedek Office** was conferred by oath. In the priesthood of Levi there was no oath, because the position was received strictly by descent. Levi was subject to death, but Melchizedek has endless life. Hebrews 7:8 says: "*And here men that die receive tithes; but there he receiveth them, of whom it is witnessed that he liveth.*" Hebrew 7:11 says: "*If therefore perfection were by the Levitical priesthood, (for under it the people received the law,) what further need was there that another priest should rise after the order of Melchizedek, and not be called after the order of Aaron?*" Levi administered the law, but Melchizedek blesses with bread and wine. Don't confuse the four categories of the law. The Levites administered all four categories of the law, because they were by calling the administrators appointed by God in the Old Testament. Those other three categories of law are still in effect today, which are. Commandments, Statutes and Judgments. The Law of Ordinances has come to an abrupt end. When King Henry VIII started the Church of England and ended the authority of the Roman Catholic Church in England, he took out all the stone altars and put in wooden tables. Why. A stone altar is where they executed the mass every time they met. They were crucifying the Son of God afresh every time they met. He put in wooden tables with bread and wine so they could serve the people. What he did was representative of the great change taking place in our civilization. This change was from the apostate Levitical Order being carried on in the Roman Catholic Church and was changed into the Melchizedek Order where the priests served the people bread and wine.

In Hebrews 7 it says that the Levitical Order had many priests but the Melchizedek Order has only one priest at any given time. We are part of the Melchizedek Order functioning under the Head Priest, who is Jesus Christ, the High Priest of the Melchizedek Order. We are organically connected to the Head and are part of His body. Being that He is Melchizedek, if you say, "I want your head to stand up" the whole body stands up. When we exalt the Head, the whole body is exalted and lifted up. Paul tells us in Colossians that Christ is the Head of all things. His pre-eminence is above all power, principalities, and the demons in and out of hell. Principalities of the air and spiritual wickedness in high places are under the dominion of Christ. We are organically connected with Him and someday we will see all enemies put under His feet and our feet.

Somebody must be the foot company. Somebody has to be the ankle company, the leg company, the knee company, because His enemies are going to be put under His foot. The Head begins the work, but the feet will smash the enemies. The Head does not get down there, but the foot does the smashing. We are organically connected to Him and are a part of His body.

In verses 21 and 25 we read that Melchizedek is a priest forever. In verse 23, Levi is described as a priest only until death. Levi held a changeable priesthood. (Hebrews 7:11-12). In verse 24 we read: *"But this man, because he continueth ever, hath an unchangeable priesthood."* The Melchizedek priesthood never changes. According to Hebrews 7:11 and 19, the Levitical Order was imperfect because Levi was an imperfect man. The Melchizedek Order was and is the perfect priestly order. Hebrews 7:27 says. *"Who needeth not daily, as those high priests, to offer up sacrifice, first for his own sins, and then for the people's: for this he did once, when he offered up himself."*

Levi had to offer up many animal sacrifices for his own self, and then for the people, but Melchizedek died once, when He offered up Himself.

Hebrews 7:28 - Levi had infirmities or weaknesses: *"For the law maketh men high priests which have infirmity; but the word of the oath, which was since the law, maketh the Son, who is consecrated for evermore."* The priests had physical infirmities. They had one requirement in order to serve as priests. They had to be perfect in their body, without apparent physical defects. In Hebrews 7:26 it says that Jesus the perfect priest was consecrated forever. *"For such an high priest became us, who is holy, harmless, undefiled, separate from sinners, and made higher than the heavens."* That applies only to the Melchizedek order. He was holy, harmless, undefiled and separate from sinners and made higher.

DAVID AS MELCHISEDEK

In I Samuel 16:1 we find an account describing the calling and anointing of David: *"And the LORD said unto Samuel, How long wilt thou mourn for Saul, seeing I have rejected him from reigning over Israel? fill thine horn with oil, and go, I will send thee to Jesse the Bethlehemite: for I have provided me a king among his sons."* In the last part of this verse it says, *"I have provided me a king."* David was of the tribe of Judah. He was the head of the dynasty of the House of David, chosen no doubt, before his birth. That was his calling. He was God's choice. Then verse twelve describes his anointing: *"And he sent, and brought him in. Now he was ruddy, and withal of a beautiful countenance, and goodly to look to. And the LORD said, Arise, anoint him: for this is he."*

Samuel did not have a choice. We know what Samuel's choice would have been: one of David's older brothers. Samuel judged them all by their outward appearance. *"Then Samuel took the horn of oil, and anointed him in the midst of his brethren: and the Spirit of the LORD came upon David from that day forward. So Samuel rose up, and went to Ramah"* (I Sam. 16:13). Why in the midst of his brethren. This was the man who would serve his brethren. He was going to serve them bread and wine. The verse continues, *"and the Spirit of the LORD came upon David from that day forward."* That was his Melchizedek anointing. Later when David was running from King Saul, he did something that was forbidden for any non-authorized man to do. **David ate the Tabernacle shewbread.** In verse 6 it says: *"So the priest gave him hallowed bread: for there was no bread there but the shewbread, that was taken from before the LORD, to put hot bread in the day when it was taken away."* David did not have a right to this holy bread, for he was not a priest. He was not a Levite.

The New Testament account in Mark 2:23-28 says. *"And it came to pass, that he [Jesus] went through the corn fields on the sabbath day; and his disciples began, as they went, to pluck the ears of corn. And the Pharisees said unto him, Behold, why do they on the sabbath day that which is not lawful? And he said unto them, Have ye never read what David did, when he had need, and was an hungred, he, and they that were with him? How he went into the house of God in the days of Abiathar the high priest, and did eat the shewbread, which is not lawful to eat but for the priests, and gave also to them which were with him? And he said unto them, The sabbath was made for man, and not man for the sabbath: Therefore the Son of man is Lord also of the sabbath."* **Jesus did not condemn His disciples for** *plucking the corn on the Sabbath, nor did He condemn David for eating the shewbread.*

In I Chronicles 15:1-2, we read where **David appointed Levites for worship and sacred service:** *"And David made him houses in the city of David, and prepared a place for the ark of God, and pitched for it a tent. Then David said, None ought to carry the ark of God but the Levites: for them hath the LORD chosen to carry the ark of God, and to minister unto him for ever."* Verse 16 says: *"And David spake to the chief of the Levites to appoint their brethren to be the singers with instruments of musick, psalteries and harps and cymbals sounding, by lifting up the voice with joy."* What was David doing getting involved in the work of the priests? It was because he was a "priest." He told the Levites, 'You appoint your brethren and get all your singers together.' Why didn't Abiathar do that. He was the High Priest. But no, David did it.

David also wore a linen ephod which was only for the priest. In II Samuel 6:13 it says: *"And it was so, that when they that bare the ark of the LORD had gone six paces, he sacrificed oxen and fatlings. And David danced before the LORD with all his might; and David was girded with a linen ephod."* That is the garment of the Levitical priest. Why is David wearing it? Why didn't the Lord strike him dead.

David also authorized sacrifices in verse 13. In I Chronicles 16:1 it says, *"So they brought the ark of God, and set it in the midst of the tent that David had pitched for it: and they offered burnt sacrifices and peace offerings before God."* They set the Ark of the Covenant in David's tent. Here it appears there was a crossover between the office of king and priest, for now King David was involved in the priestly work. Verse two says: *"And when David had made an end of offering the burnt offerings and the peace offerings, he blessed the people in the name of the LORD."* The Melchizedek ministry is for 'blessing' and now **David blessed the people.** We read in 16:3: "*And he dealt to every one of Israel, both man and woman, to every one a loaf of bread, and a good piece of flesh, and a flagon of wine."* David authorized giving to the people bread and wine. That was a Melchizedek responsibility.

We also realize that David **was a liar.** There is no need to beat around the bush about it. He lied. **He was guilty of adultery and even of murder.** Why didn't the Lord strike him dead for any one of those egregious sins. That was David the *man* who was lying, committing adultery and committing murder. That sin lived with him and remained in his record. All through the prophets this sin is mentioned. But he had a calling. Despite his imperfections, he served as an imperfect symbolic representation of Christ. Imperfect as he was, he was still a type of Christ from the tribe of Judah as had been prophesied. The record tells us that Jesus Christ Himself, the Branch, the offshoot of that stalk of Jesse came out of the root of David. In fact, He is known as the Root of David. These sins of David proved his humanity, but did not cancel out his Melchisedek authority.

The Death of the Old Order
Chapter Five

O nly Faith can understand that: God hides His *power* in weakness; His *wisdom* in folly. His *goodness* in severity; His *justice* in wrath and His *mercy* in anger. This is the foolishness of the cross. The Greeks thought the cross and its meaning was foolish and to the Jews it was a stumbling block, but unto us who believe it is the power of God.

We know that the Melchizedek priesthood existed a long time before the Levitical priesthood was established. The Levitical priesthood was only temporary, but the Melchizedek priesthood is still in existence. The Levitical priesthood was ordained by God, came in at a certain time and was terminated at a certain time, but the Melchizedek priesthood lives on as an eternal establishment. The Melchizedek priesthood is dual, encompassing the roles of both King and Priest. Our Lord and Savior is now the Melchizedek Priest, high above all others. The book of Hebrews says, *"above thy fellows."* He is high above all other fellow priests. When a weak priesthood is in office, a weak sacrifice results, but when a strong priesthood is in office, its sacrifice is all-encompassing. So when the weakness of the Levitical Order or the sacrificial system of laws was in place it signified a weak priesthood. Carnal men were executing the ordinances of God. When the Melchizedek priesthood arose, a perfect priesthood resulted through the perfect priest, Jesus Christ. **The perfection of the priest produces perfection of the sacrifice.**

Why do churches have so many problems? Why do they have church splits and some ministers go bad. It is because they are carnal men executing the ordinances of God. In other words carnal men are trying to execute sacred things even though they are not perfect. They are weak just as were the Levitical priests of the Old Testament. Weak priests and weak sacrifices preceded the perfection of the perfect King/Priest, Jesus Christ, who comes only through the Melchizedek Order.

You may say, "Well, it was prophesied that God would always have a priest before Him and that was the priesthood of Aaron." When I refer to the Law I am referring to one portion of the Law; that is of ordinances, sacrifices and ceremonies, and not to the moral commandments, judicial statutes and judgments. One of our problems with our present society is that society rejects the very idea of any authority: the Law of God, the **statutes, commandments** and **judgments**. Those three categories are still in effect today, but the fourth category, that of **ordinances, rituals** and **ceremonies** has been abolished.

In Exodus 40 we read about the consecration of the Levitical priests. What happened to the Levitical or the Aaronic priesthood. Exodus 40:12: *"And thou shalt bring Aaron and his sons unto the door of the tabernacle of the congregation, and wash them with water. And thou shalt put upon Aaron the holy garments, and anoint him, and sanctify him; that he may minister unto me in the priest's office. And thou shalt bring his sons, and clothe them with coats: And thou shalt anoint them, as thou didst anoint their father, that they may minister unto me in the priest's office: for **their anointing** shall surely be an* *everlasting priesthood throughout their generations.*" It did not say that the ordinance of the Levitical priest or the genealogy of the tribe of Levi would always be the ministers unto God. Rather it said, the **anointing** of their priesthood would be everlasting. That was the calling or the service of their priesthood.

Some say we need to reinstate the tribe of Levi in order to execute righteousness today, and that is what Orthodox Judaism is doing and many Christians are going along with it. Many young Jewish Rabbis when in training say they have discovered that they are of the tribe of Levi. They are excited, thinking they are the tribe of Levi and are learning the rabbinical law and are getting ready to reestablish the temple. Then they go into blood sacrifice and claim that they are keeping the old law of ordinances. Moses was told by the Lord that the **anointing** of the sons, not the genealogy of the sons of Aaron was what was needed for the priesthood. What did Levi deal with. What did the law of sacrifices deal with. It dealt with the sin problem and the fallen nature of man. There is nothing wrong with the Levitical **anointing** dealing with the sin problem. Somebody has to deal with the sin problem for those who are outside of salvation through Christ. It is only the *anointing* of the Levitical priesthood that remains.

Imperfect priests and imperfect sacrifices characterized the early years of the Israelite nation. Leviticus 9:1-2 reiterates that: *"And it came to pass on the eighth day, that Moses called Aaron and his sons, and the elders of Israel; And he said unto Aaron, Take thee a young calf for a sin offering, and a ram for a burnt offering, without blemish, and offer them before the LORD."* Verses 7 and 8: *"And Moses said unto Aaron, Go unto the altar, and offer thy sin offering, and thy burnt offering, and make an atonement for thyself, and for the people: and offer the offering of the people, and make an atonement for them; as the LORD commanded. Aaron therefore went unto the altar, and slew the calf of the sin offering, which was for himself.*" Aaron and his sons were imperfect priests and therefore they required all these different sacrifices. The Book of Leviticus shows that the scene must have been a bloody mess. They sacrificed thousands of animals every day and they were still insufficient. They could not atone for sin nor change the hearts of men.

In Acts 15, which quotes from the 9th chapter of the Book of Amos, we are told by James that the Holy Ghost is restoring something. "*And after they had held their peace, James answered, saying, Men and brethren, hearken unto me. Simeon* [Peter] hath *declared how God at the first did visit the Gentiles, to take out of them a people for his name. And to this agree the words of the prophets; as it is written, After this* [after He had visited the Gentiles which were the ten lost tribes of Israel and showed them salvation] *I will return, and will build again the tabernacle of David, which is fallen down; and I will build again the ruins thereof, and I will set it up:*" (Acts 15:13-15).

Is the Holy Spirit restoring the Tabernacle of David, the tabernacle of Moses or the temple of Solomon? The Tabernacle of David is clearly indicated. According to the Biblical record, the Holy Ghost has not come to restore the Levitical Order in the Tabernacle of Moses. Sometimes we have lifted Moses up higher than Jesus Christ. We focus our attention on the Tabernacle of Moses and Jesus is left in a corner somewhere. It's because we don't understand the difference between the Tabernacle of Moses and the Tabernacle of David. The Tabernacle of Moses was that tabernacle which held the Holy Place, the Most Holy Place and all the furniture in its special order. This tabernacle was temporary and by its very nature could be moved as the nation Israel moved about on their journey through the wilderness to the Promised Land.

Later David built a tabernacle that held the Ark of the Covenant. The Holy Ghost in the book of Amos, repeated in the book of Acts, says *"I am going to restore the Tabernacle of David."* (Amos 9:11). This is a dual Tabernacle because David held both offices, king and priest, while Moses held only one office: priest. The wilderness tabernacle functioned only for Moses' priesthood. Neither did the Holy Ghost through James say that He was restoring the magnificent temple of Solomon. This was the greatest temple in the world with all of its glory and riches, a permanent dwelling built of stone. It was a large and costly dwelling crafted of stone and gold, whereas the tabernacle of David was made of less expensive material. In its function, calling, service and perpetuity this unpretentious building was much greater than the Temple of Solomon.

The Old Testament tells us in Jeremiah 7:1-4: *"The word that came to Jeremiah from the LORD, saying, Stand in the gate of the LORD'S house,* [that was Solomon's temple] *and proclaim there this word, and say, Hear the word of the LORD, all ye of Judah, that enter in at these gates to worship the LORD. Thus saith the LORD of hosts, the God of Israel, Amend your ways and your doings, and I will cause you to dwell in this place. Trust ye not in lying words, saying,* [what were the lying words?] *The temple of the LORD, The temple of the LORD, The temple of the LORD, are these."* The temple was everything to these people. What this prophecy is actually saying is; 'Look at this magnificent temple. It was instituted by God, the plans were given to Solomon and he built this magnificent edifice which was one of the wonders of the world. Surely God is with us, in spite of the fact that we have violated His ways, laws, and commandments. We have broken His heart, but look at this magnificent edifice that we have here. We are going to bask in this glory and find our pride and all of our joy in this religious order that has been set up here.'

They have put all of their confidence in this religious system, because the temple was the center of religious and civil life and every other aspect of society in the Israelite civilization. So therefore they repeated, "The temple of the Lord, the temple of the Lord, the temple of the Lord." The Lord said these are nothing but empty and lying words. They put their confidence in a system that was really rotten to the core, yet they had all the outward show of their religious system. They had the Holy Place, Most Holy Place, brazen altar, courtyard, beautiful curtains, beautiful gate, all the priests wearing their consecrated garments, anointed and holy, going through a routine of rote ceremonies, thinking they had it made. They had the temple of the Lord, didn't they. Everything was fine. How could it be otherwise.

PERVERTED PRIESTHOOD

Which priestly system became perverted and was the means to Pharisaical bondage? Was it Melchizedek or Levitical. Which priestly system became perverted and became known as Talmudism and

Judaism? The sinful Jews couldn't touch the Melchizedek Order, but they could touch that earthly order. Look at the history of the denominational churches. They have a wonderful history, but where are they today? Drive through town and see all the wonderful church edifices, representing plenty of money. Jesus would have called them whited sepulchers full of dead men's bones, as He did the Pharisees in His day. Many wonderful people belong to the churches, but it is the institutional structures that become corrupt. They say, "This is the way it is done, this is what we believe, it can be done no other way. Challenge us and you will be locked out. The Holy Ghost does not belong here, we have it all figured out." God deliver us from such religious systems.

The Lord said, "Come out of her, my people." For what reason? "That ye be not partaker of her sins." Which priestly system criticized, judged and eventually condemned our Lord to death. It was the very system instituted at Mt. Sinai. How could such a wonderful, pure, God-given system, 1483 years later condemn the very Lord of Glory to death.

When the Levitical priesthood, sent their temple guards, (The Roman soldiers did not go into the Garden) they went out there to arrest Jesus. They said; "We are going to put Him on trial. 'Our' law says He must be condemned, but He was the source of Law. Their law went from holy to profane. In the hands of unholy men the God-given law went from sacred to vile. Such a priestly system today is the means of people's harsh, merciless judgment of others, regarding their ideas of religious requirements and activities based upon their Law. We can become very critical of others, severe in our attitude and bitter in our spirit, but the Melchizedek Order says, "I want to serve you with bread and wine. I don't want to judge you." The Pharisees became so harsh, so mean in their attitude of self-righteousness, they said, 'I am glad I am not like this other fellow over here.' Remember the story Jesus told. In the temple, the Publican was beating his breast, saying 'Lord be merciful to me a sinner,' while the Pharisee said, 'I am glad I am not like him.' Jesus asked, 'Which man went away justified?'. Here stands this Pharisee with all of his learning and false spirituality making a false pretense and Jesus said it was a stench; an abomination. They not only kept the Law and followed it to the letter, but they went beyond it, adding to it, and teaching as doctrine the commandments of men. Basically, Jesus was referring to the Talmud which came out of Babylon.

The Pharisees were so self-righteous and held the people in so much bondage that they would come by their homes just before the Sabbath and inspect the furniture arrangement in the home. You could not move a chair or you would be charged with bearing a burden on the Sabbath. If they came by at the end of the Sabbath and the people had moved a chair, they said, 'We did not pick it up, we just dragged it from one place to another,' the Pharisees would see the little furrows left in the ground by the chair legs and then condemn them for plowing. They took sacred things and made them profane and usually it was for selfish gain, and not just for money, but for power.

The **Levitical Order** could not purge the conscience from dead works, but the **Melchizedek Order** can. Jesus did so many miracles on the Sabbath, and many of them caused Him problems with the

Pharisees. See Matthew 12:1-8: *"At that time Jesus went on the sabbath day through the corn; and his disciples were an hungred, and began to pluck the ears of corn, and to eat. But when the Pharisees saw it, they said unto him, Behold, thy disciples do that which is not lawful to do upon the sabbath day. But he said unto them, Have ye not read what David did, when he was an hungred, and they that were with him; How he entered into the house of God, and did eat the shewbread, which was not lawful for him to eat, neither for them which were with him, but only for the priests. Or have ye not read in the law, how that on the sabbath days the priests in the temple profane the sabbath, and are blameless? But I say unto you, That in this place is one greater than the temple."*

Jesus is saying to these Pharisees, ***"I am greater than the Law."*** Jesus was greater than the ordinances and the priesthood that the Pharisees were supposedly protecting. *"But if ye had known what this meaneth, I will have mercy, and not sacrifice, ye would not have condemned the guiltless. For the Son of man is Lord even of the sabbath day."* Jesus was greater than the Sabbath. Verse 41 says: *"The men of Nineveh shall rise in judgment with this generation, and shall condemn it: because they repented at the preaching of Jonas; and, behold, a greater than Jonas is here.* **Jesus was greater than the prophetic order.** *The queen of the south shall rise up in the judgment with this generation, and shall condemn it: for she came from the uttermost parts of the earth to hear the wisdom of Solomon; and, behold, a greater than Solomon is here."*

Jesus *was* **greater than the kingly order and the temple**. He is greater than Jonah, who represented the ***prophetic order*** in the Old Testament and greater than Solomon who represented the **kingly order**. The examples Jesus gave here illustrate the offices of Prophet, Priest and King. Jesus said that He was greater than all three of them. The Lord of Glory is now among us. He is God in flesh. The Pharisees stand in their pious robes of self-righteousness saying, 'Who is this fellow over here. We have this temple, the sacred writing of the prophets, and this kingly order of the Solomon is among us.' But they did not recognize the Lord of Glory who was standing right there and who was the personification and fulfillment of all three of these sacred roles.

Sometimes the Lord will let us run our political or religious system all of our lifetime and all the while He is standing back just watching. He is not a part of it. The Lord will let you run a religious order and even allow tremendous growth, but He may not be a part of it.

JESUS

Three men in the New Testament got in trouble for proclaiming the death of the old Levitical Order. The first was Jesus. In Matthew 26:59 we read the account of a religious trial. Jesus suffered religious and civil trials for a total of six. This trial took place before Caiaphas the High Priest where the Scribes and Elders were assembled. "*Now the chief priests, and elders, and all the council, sought false witness against Jesus, to put him to death; But found none: yea, though many false witnesses came, yet found they none. At the last came two false witnesses, And said, This fellow said, I am able to destroy the temple of God, and to build it in three days.*" Now that was a 'no-no' to say that the temple of Solomon would be destroyed. The temple was considered sacred as was cited by Jeremiah when he said: *"the Temple, the Temple, the Temple of the Lord."*

The religious order was held to be sacred, but God had already moved on. God cannot be confined; you can only fence where He has been, He is no longer there. When you put a sign up, "This is the greatest and latest," He has already gone on. This site has become nothing but a monument and a memorial. It first begins as a memorial of what God has done, and then it turns into a monument and then a mausoleum full of dead works. Matthew 27:39-40; *"And they that passed by reviled him, wagging their heads, And saying, Thou that destroyest the temple, and buildest it in three days, save thyself. If thou be the Son of God, come down from the cross."* They compared the temple or religious order of Levi to the Son of God Himself. 'You say you are the Son of God? You say you are going to rebuild the temple?' Those were the words of blind religious leaders.

John 2:18-19: *"Then answered the Jews and said unto him, What sign shewest thou unto us, seeing that thou doest these things? Jesus answered and said unto them, Destroy this temple, and in three days I will raise it up."* What is He destroying. Not that physical temple standing before them. Verse 20: *"Then said the Jews, Forty and six years was this temple in building, and wilt thou rear it up in three days? But he spake of the temple of his body."* Luke 19:41-44: *"And when he was come near, he beheld the city, and wept over it, Saying, If thou hadst known, even thou, at least in this thy day, the things which belong unto thy peace! but now they are hid from thine eyes. For the days shall come upon thee, that thine enemies shall cast a trench about thee,* [talking about the Roman armies] *and compass thee round, and keep thee in on every side, And shall lay thee even with the ground, and thy children within thee; and they shall not leave in thee one stone upon another; because thou knewest not the time of thy visitation."* Jesus was the grand visitor and they did not recognize Him. Preoccupied with their previous learning, ideas and religious order, they missed the visitation of God in flesh. Jesus was accused of blasphemy, because He spoke against idolizing the temple.

STEPHEN

The next man who spoke against the temple was Stephen. In Acts 6:8-14, we read: *"And Stephen, full of faith and power, did great wonders and miracles among the people. Then there arose certain of the synagogue, which is called the synagogue of the Libertines, and Cyrenians, and Alexandrians, and of them of Cilicia and of Asia, disputing with Stephen. And they were not able to resist the wisdom and the spirit by which he spake. Then they suborned men, which said, We have heard him speak blasphemous words against Moses, and against God. And they stirred up the people, and the elders, and the scribes, and came upon him, and caught him, and brought him to the council, And set up false witnesses, which said, This man ceaseth not to speak blasphemous words against this holy place, and the law: For we have heard him say, that this Jesus of Nazareth shall destroy this place, and shall change the customs which Moses delivered us."* The Jewish chief priests and Pharisees could not bear the idea that their customs would be changed. The very thought was intolerable to them.

PAUL

The third man to be accused of profaning the temple was Paul. Accusations were made against Paul by the Jewish leaders when he appeared before Governor Felix in Acts 24:6: *"Who also hath gone about to profane the temple. whom we took, and would have judged according to our law..."* Then in Acts 21:28: *"Crying out, Men of Israel, help: This is the man, that teacheth all men every where 1) against the* people *2) and the law, 3) and this place: and* **(4)** *further brought Greeks also into the temple, and hath polluted this holy place."* They said, 'Those people don't belong in here. We have set up the guidelines for who may be admitted to the temple and who cannot.' What hypocritical self-righteousness. Stephen as a prophet said, *"God is going to destroy this place."* God destroyed that old religious, priestly system that they relied upon.

What we need today is Jesus Christ in all of His glory to destroy our man made religious shrines. Man wants to worship God according to his own mental concepts of God. He wants to make visible images of Him. The most effective way to desecrate and destroy something true is to externalize it into graven images made with hands, or by ceremonies created by the thoughts, well intentioned designs of men. The Apostle Paul probably wouldn't be invited into many churches today and maybe Jesus wouldn't be invited into them either. We need to pray; "Lord, rip the old Levitical system out of me whereby I rely on the old order of what I was raised in or the things whereby I have found comfort in my religious box. Lord, make me into a person made in Your own image. Reveal unto me the reality that is Yourself."

The Old Testament prophets pointed back to the Exodus, the coming out of Egypt. We see something greater than the Exodus and that is Calvary; someone greater than Moses and that is Jesus. Moses brought the people out of bondage, but he couldn't take them into the Promised Land. Moses was weak. He had fears and apprehensions. He had a little dispute with the Lord and said, "I can't do this." He was just a man. Moses was at the first Passover, but I don't think Moses ever celebrated the Feast of Tabernacles. He did not even enter into Canaan land.

In Hebrew. 3:1-6 the writer describes this: *"Wherefore, holy brethren. partakers of the heavenly calling, consider the Apostle and High Priest of our profession, Christ Jesus; Who was faithful to him that appointed him, as also Moses was faithful in all his house. For this man was counted worthy of more glory than Moses, inasmuch as he who hath builded the house hath more honour than the house. For every house is builded by some man; but he that built all things is God. And Moses verily was faithful in all his house as a servant, for a testimony of those things which were to be spoken after*; [They were only a shadow, a type of things to come.] *But Christ as a son over his own house; whose house are we, if we hold fast the confidence and the rejoicing of the hope firm unto the end."* Christ is the Son over His own house, and we are His house. He is building us. We need church order and structure, and not chaos, but sometimes church structure can move the Lord of Glory outside the door, into a place of insignificance. He really wants to build and bring us into maturity into the full stature of the fullness of the measure of Christ.

In Acts 15:1-2 it says: *"And certain men which came down from Judaea taught the brethren, and said, Except ye be circumcised after the manner of Moses, ye cannot be saved. When therefore Paul and Barnabas had no small dissension and disputation with them, they determined that Paul and Barnabas, and certain other of them, should go up to Jerusalem unto the apostles and elders about this question."* This tells us there were Judaizers in that day. They said, oh yes, we believe in the grace of God, BUT you had better be circumcised. What did that bring. Dissension. It was leaven in the lump. It goes everywhere. They came down from Judaea and taught the brethren and no doubt preached a wonderful message, but then included the thought that you must return to the Law of Moses if you really want to be saved. Sad to say, I think I have heard that in our day.

THE ONE PERFECT PERSON

In Acts 15:19-21 it says: *"Wherefore my sentence is, that we trouble not them, which from among the Gentiles are turned to God: But that we write unto them, that they abstain from pollutions of idols, and from fornication, and from things strangled, and from blood. For Moses of old time hath in every city them that preach him, being read in the synagogues every sabbath day."*

Paul told the chief priests and scribes that there was one greater than Moses and he quickly found himself on a ship headed for Rome. He was accused of blaspheming the temple, the holy place, and the law. Do you think he was really blaspheming the law. He was rather trying to show them a more perfect way. The religious order was composed of the very men who sent him to Rome where

Nero ordered his beheading. This happened as he traveled on the Ostian Way, outside the city of Rome. His unforgivable transgression was that he was trying to tell the people there was someone greater than Moses.

We need a living reality to bring power into our lives; something that can purge our conscience of dead works. That has come to us in the **Melchizedek Order, executed by one perfect Person.** That is Jesus Christ Himself. The record tells us: *"be it known unto you, therefore, men and brethren, that through this man is preached the forgiveness of sins and by Him all that believe are justified from all things from which we could not be justified by the law of Moses."* He was talking about the law of ordinances and not the law of commandments, judgments and statutes. These did not justify either, but the law of ordinances dealt specifically with the sin problem during its jurisdiction.

What does the word 'ordinance' mean in this case. It means to subscribe by statute, to submit to certain rule or an equitable deed, a statute or decision giving justification or righteousness. In Hebrews 9:1-5 we read: *"Then verily the first covenant had also ordinances of divine service, and a worldly sanctuary. For there was a tabernacle made; the first, wherein was the candlestick, and the table, and the shewbread; which is called the sanctuary. And after the second veil, the tabernacle which is called the Holiest of all; Which had the golden censer, and the ark of the covenant overlaid round about with gold, wherein was the golden pot that had manna, and Aaron's rod that budded, and the tables of the covenant; And over it the cherubims of glory shadowing the mercyseat; of which we cannot now speak particularly."*

When we read the Old Testament, we revere it. It is the foundation of our faith, but it tells us in Hebrews 9:6-7: *"Now when these things were thus ordained, the priests went always into the first tabernacle, accomplishing the service of God. But into the second went the high priest alone once every year, not without blood, which he offered for himself, and for the errors of the people:"* In verse 8 the Holy Ghost is signifying something to us, namely, that the way into the Holiest of all was not yet known in the Old Covenant. That became known only in the New Covenant. Verse 9 tells us that it was only *"a figure for the time then present, in which were offered both gifts and sacrifices, that could not make him that did the service perfect, as pertaining to the conscience;"* It could not change the conscience or spirit man, because that order *"Which stood only in meats and drinks, and divers washings, and carnal ordinances, imposed on them until the time of reformation."* That reformation was the coming of the Messiah and His death. The old order was imposed on the people, but it was cancelled by Jesus Christ.

The Apostle Paul in Colossians 2:.11-17 wrote: *"In whom also ye are circumcised with the circumcision made without hands, in putting off the body of the sins of the flesh by the circumcision of Christ: Buried with him in baptism, wherein also ye are risen with him through the faith of the operation of God, who hath raised him from the dead." And you, being dead in your sins and the uncircumcision of your flesh, hath he quickened together with him, having forgiven you all trespasses. Blotting out the handwriting of ordinances that was against us, which was contrary to us, and took it out of the way, nailing it to his cross.* [He nailed the laws of ordinances to the cross] *And having spoiled principalities and powers,* [In this context he was talking about the religious laws of ordinances that were established under Moses, that became contrary to the best interests of the people and produced bondage that was later formalized as Talmudism or Judaism. He says He spoiled them or destroyed their religious system.] *he made a shew of them openly, triumphing over them in it. Let no man therefore judge you in meat, or in drink, or in respect of an holyday, or of the new moon, or of the sabbath days. Which are a shadow of things to come; but the body is of Christ."*

The Levitical religious order told the people where to worship, how to worship and when to worship. They had to do each ritual at a certain place and at a certain time. Therefore the temple officials judged the people and instituted their religious activities according to a calendar. If we cannot celebrate the feast days: Passover, Firstfruits, Unleavened Bread, Pentecost, Trumpets, Atonement and Tabernacles in a higher realm, which is the Melchizedek Priesthood, then don't do it at all. **Jesus is our worship location, worship timeframe and** worship **director.** He is the Passover. He is the Melchizedek priest who is continually serving bread and wine to His people. The Feast no longer must be held only on the 14th or 15th day of Abib each year. Jesus is our Resurrection and our Firstfruits. Paul talked about the Feast of Unleavened Bread in I Corinthians 5:6-8 and said: *"Your glorying is not good. Know ye not that a little leaven leaveneth the whole lump? Purge out therefore the old leaven, that ye may be a new lump, as ye are unleavened. For even Christ our passover is sacrificed for us. Therefore let us keep the feast, not with old leaven, neither with the leaven of malice and wickedness; but with the unleavened bread of sincerity and truth."*

In John 4:19-23 we read the story of the woman at the well: *"The woman saith unto him, Sir, I perceive that thou art a prophet. Our fathers worshipped in **this** mountain; and ye say, that in Jerusalem is the place where men ought to worship. Jesus saith unto her, Woman, believe me, the hour cometh, when ye shall neither in this mountain, nor yet at Jerusalem, worship the Father. Ye worship ye know not what: we know what we worship: for salvation is of the Jews. But the hour cometh, and now is, when the true worshippers shall worship the Father in spirit and in truth."* Jesus did not say to worship at this mountain at this particular time of the year, but a true worshiper worships in spirit. He worships in truth, in a higher order. Levi says you have to go through certain religious activities, but Melchizedek says come up higher and worship Me in the Spirit.

We can go through our rituals and call them anything we want to call them, but they will amount to nothing. We can call our meetings Passover, Pentecost, Tabernacles and there are no better names to call them because they are the names that God ordained in the Old Testament, but we do not commemorate or celebrate them according to the old law. We celebrate them in fulfillment. Jesus is our Passover, our Firstfruits and our Unleavened Bread. It's better to **experience Pentecost** than hold the celebration of a past event. The same is true for Atonement, Trumpets and Tabernacles. Tabernacles mean that He comes to continually abide in us, God in flesh. He is the true Tabernacle, far beyond just holding a series of meetings and calling them Tabernacles.

The New Priesthood
Chapter Six

The faithful High Priest described in Psalm 40:6 is a prophetic statement concerning Jesus Christ and His sacrifice. The prophecy goes beyond His sacrifice and talks about Him as a person, calling and anointing. His sacrifice was actually based upon His righteousness. The fulfillment is given in Hebrews 10:5-9. The Hebrews passage is almost an exact copy of Psalm 40:6-10: *"Wherefore when he cometh into the world, he saith, Sacrifice and offering thou wouldest not, but a body hast thou prepared me. In burnt offerings and sacrifices for sin thou hast had no pleasure.* [no satisfaction] *Then said I, Lo, I come (in the volume of the book it is written of me,) to do thy will, O God. Above when he said. Sacrifice and offering and burnt offerings and offering for sin thou wouldest not, neither hadst pleasure therein; which are offered by the law; Then said he, Lo, I come to do thy will, O God. He taketh away the first, that he may establish the second."* We need to catch a greater vision of the perfect sacrifice of Jesus Christ. Throughout our Christian experience we will probably hear very few sermons on the perfection of Jesus Christ or the 100% effectiveness of His work on the cross. He fulfilled all the stipulations of the Levitical requirements for a perfect sacrifice, yet that was a sacrifice of the blood of animals: of bulls, goats and lambs. Jesus' sacrifice was a perfect sacrifice as He gave His own sinless body.

The writer of Hebrews gives us a description of Jesus' condescension to the level of Adam's existence. Hebrews 2:1-4: *"Therefore we ought to give the more earnest heed to the things which we have heard, lest at any time we should let them slip. For if the word spoken by angels was steadfast, and every transgression and disobedience received a just recompense of reward; How shall we escape, if we neglect so great salvation; which at the first began to 1) be spoken by the Lord, and 2) was confirmed unto us by them that heard him; God also bearing them* [the Apostles] *witness, both with signs and wonders, and with divers* [a variety of many] *miracles, and gifts of the Holy Ghost, according to his own will?"* [not the will of the disciples]. Heb. 2:5: *"For unto the angels hath he not put in subjection the world to come, whereof we speak. But one in a certain place* (Psalm 8) *testified, saying, What is man, that thou art mindful of him? or the son of man, that thou visitest him. Thou madest him* [man] *a little lower than the angels; thou crownedst him with glory and honour, and didst set him over the works of thy hands. Thou hast put all things in subjection under his feet. For in that he put all in subjection under him, he left nothing that is not put under him. But now we see not yet all things put under him. But we see Jesus, who was made a little lower than the angels for the suffering of death, crowned with glory and honour; that he by the grace of God should taste death for every man."*

Why was Jesus made a little lower than the angels. The writer is talking about man being made lower than the angels. Then we see Jesus also made a little lower than the angels. Jesus in His humanity was brought to the same level as man. He was 100% man. He took on the form of Abraham so that He could identify with the children of Abraham. He was called one of our brethren. Heb.

84

2:9 *"But we see Jesus, who was made a little lower than the angels for the suffering of death, crowned with glory and honour; that he by the grace of God should taste death for every* [Adam] *man."* In Adam all died, but in Christ all Adam is made alive.

Heb. 2:10: *"For it became him, for whom are all things, and by whom are all things, in bringing many sons unto glory, to make the captain of their salvation perfect through sufferings."* All things were created for Him. This writer says, *"for whom all things, and by whom."* He created them for His own pleasure and in bringing many sons to glory to make the captain; originator, founder and origin of their salvation, perfect through sufferings. It seems to give the impression that Jesus had to be made perfect through trial and error. That is not the meaning of the text. To *make,* means to **prove, execute, complete, conclude, discharge, finish and bring to a close.** In John 19:30 Jesus said, *'It is finished.'* When He said, *'it is finished',* it means just that. Everything has been accomplished by the appointment of the Father as revealed in the Scriptures by the prophets that Jesus must do. Everything that was prophesied of Him, He has fulfilled. He made a perfect completion of His divine task through His suffering. It does not mean that, being imperfect, He must by trial and error in suffering be made perfect.

We have to endure such experiences because we are imperfect. He **proved** His perfection through suffering. He proved that He was already perfect by His suffering because He never faltered in His suffering. I Peter 2:21-23: *"For even hereunto were ye called: because Christ also suffered for us, leaving us an example, that ye should follow his steps. Who did no sin, neither was guile found in his mouth:*

Who, when he was reviled, reviled not again; [We as men have a tendency to fight back. He did not revile when He was reviled by others] when *he suffered, he threatened not; but committed himself to him that judgeth."* In all His suffering, He had a perfect reaction to that suffering. When reading Hebrews 2:10. read it this way, 'for it became Him, for whom are all things, and by whom are all things, in bringing many sons unto glory, **to prove the captain of their salvation was perfect through all His sufferings.'** 'Perfect' here means not only to prove but to carry out or execute. He said this in the Book of John: "Father, everything that You have given Me to do I have accomplished." This word perfect means completion. He completed everything that the Father gave Him to do. He proved His perfection through His sufferings.

Hebrews 2:11,12: *"For both he that sanctifieth and they who are sanctified are all of one*: [**one family**] *for which cause he is not ashamed to call them brethren."* [You don't call people brethren who are not in your family." *"Saying, I will declare thy name* (Psalm 22:22) unto *my brethren, in the midst of the church* [congregation] will *I sing praise unto thee. And again, I will put my trust in him. And again, Behold I and the children which God hath given me"* (Isaiah 8). This also refers back to John when Jesus called His disciples 'brethren' and in several cases He said; "Father, thou hast given them to me." So He must be talking about His own brethren. The thought goes back to verse 10 where it says, "bringing many **sons**." These are brethren He is bringing to this same state that He already possesses. Now the sons, plural, go through suffering to arrive at that state of perfection, but the pattern Son was born perfect. He lived a perfect life, reacted perfectly in all of His sufferings and died perfect. Therefore in His life He lived the life of ***His Melchizedek calling***, not the life of a Levitical calling, yet He fulfilled both.

In Hebrew. 5:1-6 it says: "*For every high priest taken from among men is ordained for men in things pertaining to God, that he may offer both gifts and sacrifices for sins:* [Levitical priests] *Who can have compassion on the ignorant, and on them that are out of the way; for that he himself also is compassed with infirmity. And by reason hereof he ought, as for the people, so also for himself, to offer for sins. And no man taketh this honour unto himself, but he that is called of God, as was Aaron. So also Christ glorified not himself to be made an high priest; but he that said unto him, Thou art my Son, today have I begotten thee. As he saith also in another place. Thou art a priest for ever after the order of Melchizedek.*"

The writer is talking about the Levitical priesthood which was a wonderful priesthood which offered gifts and sacrifices for sins, but this priesthood was not open to just anyone. He said no man takes this honor to himself. You have to be called of God as were Aaron and his sons. But a greater priest came in Christ who did not glorify Himself to be a high priest like unto Aaron. In the earthly life of Jesus Christ, He did not flaunt His authority to take over the seat of the Levitical High Priest, who was in office when He was living. He let that High Priest in all of his imperfection continue in that office. It is possible that the man holding that office at that time was not even a pure Levite. But the Lord let him hold that position, because the Lord knew it was a temporary position.

Heb. 6:6: *"Thou art a priest for ever after the order of Melchizedek. Who in the days of his flesh,* [the earthly life of our Lord] *when he had offered up prayers and supplications with strong crying and tears unto him that was able to save him from death, and was heard in that he feared; Though he were a Son, yet learned he obedience by the things which he suffered;"* He did not have to learn obedience. He proved His obedience by the things that He suffered. Though He were a son, yet He was accustomed to, or He was in the habit of, obedience in the things which He suffered. He was already accustomed to the principle of obedience before His passion during the last week of His life. Jesus was not imperfect right up to the end and then suddenly He became perfect. He was already perfect in His birth, His life and teaching. Otherwise, we would have doubt about some of the things He did and said before He became perfect.

Heb. 5:9, 10: *"And being made perfect, he became the author of eternal salvation unto all them that obey him;"* [He was not **made** perfect, He was **born** perfect.] *"Called of God an high priest after the order of Melchizedek."* He was not called after the imperfect Order of Aaron, but after the perfect Order of Melchizedek.

Hebrews 1:1-4, tells us that God at one time spoke through His prophets. **But how is He speaking today?** *"God, who at sundry times and in divers manners spake in time past unto the fathers by the prophets, Hath in these last days spoken unto us by his Son, whom he hath appointed heir of all things, by whom also he made the worlds; Who being the brightness of his glory, and the express image of his person, and upholding all things by the word of his power, when he had by himself purged our sins, sat down on the right hand of the*

Majesty on high;" That term 'sat down' means that whatever His work was, He had accomplished it. He completed it and sat down, totally satisfied that His work had been carried out according to plan. Hebrews chapter two says He was made a little *lower* than the angels, but He was made *better* than the angels. Lower because of His humanity, but better because of His perfection.

Verse 4: *"Being made so much better than the angels, as he hath by inheritance obtained a more excellent name than they."* Our Lord has by inheritance obtained a *more excellent name.* In 8:6 it tells us He has obtained a more excellent ministry: *"But now hath he obtained a more excellent ministry, by how much also he is the mediator of a better covenant, which was established upon better promises."* Why was His *ministry more excellent.* Because His name was more excellent; *His person was more excellent.* He had a more excellent name, therefore a more excellent ministry. Excellent means that it cannot get any better.

How did He obtain this great name. He obtained it by *inheritance* and by His birth. He inherited His name from His Father and by His *achievements.* His superior achievements proved His superiority. Who achieved a more excellent ministry and sacrifice. The Melchizedek Order achieved a more excellent sacrifice and ministry than the Aaronic priesthood. When we mention the name of Jesus, we are speaking a name that was given by divine authority, spoken out of the mouth of God Himself. In essence, He said to Joseph, "This is His name. You don't have the authority to name this son, I am naming Him." He received His name by inheritance from God His Father.

The Book of Hebrews in chapter six records that the writer had more to say than what he had time to write at the moment. Hebrews 6:1 says; *"Therefore leaving the principles of the doctrine of Christ, let us go on unto perfection;"* The word *'leaving'* in the Greek Lexicon, means 'not to be discussed now.' It does not mean that you forsake the doctrines of Christ. It means, temporarily the writer is not going to discuss the doctrines of Christ, but rather going to lead us into perfection; into something deeper, higher, and greater. It is not that the writer was disdaining or minimizing that which he had just mentioned, but he couldn't cover everything in his letter. Then we read this phrase, *"not laying again the foundation of repentance from dead works, and of faith toward God,"* The phrase, 'not laying again' has been another troublesome one to a lot of people. It means *'not overthrowing the foundation of repentance from dead works.'*

We are not throwing out repentance from dead works or faith towards God. That word 'foundation' is actually the same word that is used in the phrase, 'from the foundation of the world,' meaning the **overthrow** of the world or some past civilization. Not throwing down, not to put in a lower position *"the foundation of repentance from dead works or faith towards God. Of the doctrine of baptisms, and of laying on of hands, and of resurrection of the dead, and of eternal judgment."* He is saying, I am not minimizing those subjects, but I want to take you on to a great example, a perfect example of faith. This word 'perfection' in verse one means not just a thing, but a person. It is talking about the perfect person of Jesus Christ.

That Person is defined by the Lexicon as *a completer. consummator. finisher. perfecter, one who has in his own person raised faith to its perfection and thereby has set before us the highest example of faith.*" This word **perfection** is talking about a person, not just a state of being. This is what Hebrews is all about. The writer is saying; 'I don't have the time now to discuss all the doctrines of Christ. I am not going to overthrow faith in God, the repentance of sin, or eternal judgment, but what I want to do is to turn your eyes toward the Completer, the Consummator, the Finisher, the One who is perfect from the beginning and has completed His work to perfection.' That changes the text completely. Some people use this text to throw out all the basics. The writer is saying. I am not minimizing these other doctrines, but I want to point you to One who is **the perfecter, the completer, the finisher after the Order of Melchizedek.**' He could not do this after the order of Aaron.

The Melchizedek Temple
Chapter Seven

In the Book of Hebrews, thoughts and ideas arise that overlap one another. Sometimes this overlap of ideas necessitates repetition of thought and speech throughout the epistle, yet when we ponder the basic truths of the text and context, they are beyond our human comprehension. Sometimes we encounter simple concepts in God's Word, like 'Jesus wept,' and that is easily understandable; however, other truths and illustrations can be understood only through divine revelation. We can understand Jesus Christ only by God's work in us. The Apostle Paul said, "No man can call Him Lord, except by the Holy Ghost." The name of Jesus is very popular in our country and even around the world. It appears on radio, television, billboards, and on other sites both sacred and secular, but do we really understand who this Man was and is. We can't, unless we understand strictly through divine revelation. Christianity came by *divine revelation* and can be understood and accepted only by divine revelation. It is not something that came out of the heart of man, otherwise man would be able to change it. These eternal truths are intrinsic to the nature of God Himself. All religions are basically man's search for their god, except for Christianity, which is **God's search for man.** Usually religion is that set of beliefs and practices whereby man is constantly searching for his god, regardless of who that god may be. In contrast, Christianity is a divine revelation through which God is revealing Himself to man. That revelation is continually unfolding throughout history.

Hebrews 10:10: *"By the which will we are sanctified through the offering of the body of Jesus Christ once for all."* Notice the word 'body'. The Bible tells us the Word became flesh. That flesh is a Person, Jesus Christ. An erroneous belief has persisted that when Jesus died His body didn't really die, but went into a swoon state, a state of deep and unresponsive unconsciousness. What that ancient belief is trying to do is nullify the blood offering of Jesus Christ in fulfillment of all Old Testament prophecies. Therefore if the Jewish hierarchy could deny the death of Christ's body, they could also deny the resurrection of His body and its miraculous meaning. The writer tells us that *'through the offering of the body,'* (the flesh).

Verse 11: *"and every priest standeth daily ministering and offering oftentimes the same sacrifices, which can never take away sins: But this man, after he had offered one sacrifice for sins for ever, sat down on the right hand of God; From henceforth expecting till his enemies be made his footstool. For by one offering he hath perfected for ever them that are sanctified. Whereof the Holy Ghost also is a witness to us: for after that he* [the Holy Ghost] *had said before, This is the covenant that I will make with them after those days, saith the Lord, I will put my laws into their hearts,* [He didn't say He was going to do away with the law, He said He would put it in our hearts.] *and in their minds will I write them; And their sins and iniquities will I remember no more. Now where remission of these is, there is no more offering for sin."* [No more sacrifice for sins is needed] *"Having therefore, brethren, boldness to enter into the holiest by the blood of Jesus."* Our entrance into the holiest is by the blood of Jesus Christ. The qualifying entrance of the High Priest into the Most Holy Place was by the blood of bulls and goats. Blood is still the only qualifying means of entrance today.

Concerning the Levitical and the Melchizedek Order, a contrast exists between their two temples, tabernacles or dwelling places. The first tabernacle is described in Hebrews 9:1-7: "*Then verily the first covenant had also ordinances of divine service, and a worldly sanctuary. For there was a tabernacle made; the first, wherein was the candlestick, and the table, and the shewbread; which is called the sanctuary. And after the second veil, the tabernacle which is called the Holiest of all; Which had the golden censer, and the ark of the covenant overlaid round about with gold, wherein was the golden pot that had manna, and Aaron's rod that budded, and the tables of the covenant; And over it the cherubims of glory shadowing the mercy seat; of which we cannot now speak particularly. Now when these things were thus ordained,* [executed or carried out] *the priests went always into the first tabernacle, accomplishing the service of God. But into the second went the high priest alone once every year, not without blood, which he offered for himself, and for the errors of the people.*" The writer is making the distinction between the Holy Place and the Most Holy Place. When we read in the Old Testament about the temple or the tabernacle, we must distinguish which part is spoken of. The word tabernacle means **cloth hut, a place of habitation**. Usually it meant a **temporary residence**. These bodies that we now inhabit are referred to as tabernacles. They are strictly temporary. Our bodies are the dwelling place of God, but they are not the final dwelling place. It has to be changed to make it a perfect tabernacle.

THE EARTHLY AND THE HEAVENLY

In Hebrews 9:1-7 the writer is talking about the earthly tabernacle of Moses. In verse 8 he refers to another tabernacle. "*The*

Holy Ghost this signifying, [making clear] *that the way into the holiest of all was not yet made manifest, while as the first tabernacle was yet standing:"* That tells us that the first tabernacle and its furniture had to be destroyed before the Holy Ghost could make manifest the way into the true tabernacle. In our religious nature, we always love to have something visible and external. Some people wear crosses around their necks, or display pictures or other religious emblems in their homes.

They constantly need something visible in order to remind them of things that are invisible. There is a better way than that. Those visible things can automatically become a substitute. The tabernacle of Moses in the wilderness, with all its furniture, beautiful and ordained of God, became instead a religious fetish to the people. The Temple of Solomon became a religious idol. The Israelites lost sight of God who first ordained it. Their obedience meant nothing to them as long as they could go to that temple and carry out their religious exercises, making sacrifices for their sins. It made them feel real good and fuzzy on the inside, but this false worship became an abomination before God.

God could not indicate or complete the way into the holiest of all in the true tabernacle until that first tabernacle and all of its furniture was removed. **As long as the carnal tabernacle stood, the true tabernacle could not be manifested. Once the true tabernacle was manifested, the old carnal tabernacle had to go.** Jesus offered His blood in the Most Holy Place in the heavenly tabernacle, not in the one in old Jerusalem.

Moses' tabernacle decayed. Solomon's temple was built in its place and that was destroyed. It was then restored, but the glory was not in it as it had been when Solomon had dedicated that temple. Then Herod, about fifteen years before the birth of Christ, restored the reconstructed temple. The temple was central to everything in the life and civilization of Israel, but it became corrupt. Where and how did it become corrupt. The brick and mortar in themselves were not corrupt. The Temple became corrupt in their minds because of the meaning they attributed to it. This corruption results when man touches and changes the sacred things that God gave him. This tabernacle that God had ordained under Moses and the temple under Solomon had to be removed.

When Jesus walked the dusty roads of Galilee, Judea and Samaria, a temple stood in Jerusalem. This earthly temple in Jerusalem took Herod 46 years to rebuild. Jesus as a priest was not of the tribe of Levi, so He was never qualified to go into its Holy Place. As far as we know Jesus never walked into that temple's Holy Place or much less the Most Holy Place. In the flesh He was not qualified to minister there. In the Spirit He was qualified, but He did not usurp their authority. One of the reasons He did not, was that the Temple no longer held the Holy Place, for it was in the Person of Jesus Christ. *He was the Holy Place*. Out of the Holy Place came blessing and glory as He touched people and they were healed. There was the blessing and the glory. The Temple had become nothing but a religious fetish. So when Jesus offered His blood it was never carried into the Holy Place in earthly Jerusalem. *Jesus' blood never crossed the threshold of the Holy Place* in the old temple. The writer in Hebrews tells us that He offered His blood through the eternal spirit (the Holy Spirit) in the tabernacle in Heaven.

Hebrews 8:1-2 tells us: *"Now of the things which we have spoken this is the sum: We have such an high priest, who is set on the right hand of the throne of the Majesty in the heavens; A minister of the sanctuary, and of the true tabernacle, which the Lord pitched, and not man."* Apparently there must be a heavenly tabernacle, with all of its functions, and Moses was commanded to build the earthly tabernacle after this perfect pattern. Hebrews 8:5: *"Who serve unto the example and shadow of heavenly things, as Moses was admonished of God when he was about to make the tabernacle: for, See, saith he, that thou make all things according to the pattern shewed to thee in the mount."* Much confusion is present in our world today concerning the temple of God. Different words are used in the New Testament for 'temple.' **'Heiron'** means a sacred religious place and could refer even to idolatry; it could be a sacred place to the worshipers of the Artemis, or the temple of Diana. In Jerusalem the writers of the New Testament used that same Greek word to refer to the Jewish temple itself, signifying the entire structure of the temple with all of its precincts thereof, distinct from the inner sanctuary.

Then there was another word **'naos.'** That referred strictly to the Holy Place and Most Holy Place. The Bible tells us in Luke 2:27: *"And he* [Simeon] *came by the Spirit into the temple: and when the parents brought in the child Jesus, to do for him after the custom of the law,. .* It does not mean that Joseph and Mary were in the Most Holy Place. They were in one of the outer courts. In Luke 2:37, referring to Anna: *"And she was a widow of about fourscore and four years, which departed not from the temple, but served God with fastings and prayers night and day."* She did not live in the Most Holy Place or in the sanctuary. She lived in one of the living quarters inside that great edifice. Luke 2:46: *"And it came to pass, that after three days they found him* [Jesus] *in the temple, sitting in the midst of the doctors, both hearing them, and asking them questions."* Luke 19:47: *"And he taught daily in the temple."* He was in the outer courts or on the steps or entry ways, teaching the people there. Luke 20:1: *"And it came to pass, that on one of those days, as he taught the people in the temple ..."* He was not in the Holy Place. Jesus never went into the Holy Place to sanctify that place. Never! Otherwise the Melchizedek Order in which He was operating would be submitting to the Levitical Order.

This word '*naos*' means a shrine or sanctuary in the temple which only the priest could lawfully enter. Jesus being of the tribe of Judah from His physical, genealogical ancestry was not qualified to go into the Most Holy Place. That Levitical religious order had barred the One who actually established and set it up. He knew that Levitical Order was temporary and He knew that His body was the real temple. In John 2, He said; *'Destroy this temple.'* What He said and meant was one thing, but what they heard was something totally different. In their carnality they looked around, 'Oh, you mean this beautiful edifice, you're going to destroy this temple and in three days you will raise it up, you've got to be crazy.' They displayed their religious carnality. Jesus said, 'I am not talking about this building, but about the temple of My body.' **The real temple of God was Jesus in flesh.** To Judaism and the Levitical hierarchy this whole idea was very offensive. Among themselves they said, 'We have to get rid of this man.' That is one of the accusations they brought against Him at one of His six trials. They hired false witnesses who brought the accusations. Jesus was the true sacred temple, but none of the Jewish authorities recognized it.

Luke 9:31-32, tells us: "*Who appeared in glory, and spake of his decease which he should accomplish at Jerusalem. But Peter and they that were with him were heavy with sleep: and when they were awake, they saw his glory, and the two men that stood with him.*" They saw His **body.** His body had a glory that possessed a pre-glorification, pre-resurrection quality. It was a glory that was over His whole body. Why do we put such an emphasis on the body. The writer tells us in Hebrews that He took upon Himself the same form of the children of Abraham that He might identify with us. The Savior is not just a spiritual body floating around somewhere. He is not a ghost. He took upon Himself a physical body so that He could identify with the children of Abraham, even unto death. Since His body died, we die. Since His body was made alive, that is our hope. We also will be resurrected in newness of life.

The physical body of Jesus Christ was sitting at the table with His disciples. He took some bread, broke it and said, 'This is my body (of the New Covenant) which is broken. Just as you see this bread broken, my physical body is going to be broken.' He was not saying that particular bread was His body, but just as this bread is broken, My body is going to be broken for you. This temple is going to be broken. John the Revelator writes in one of his Epistles, "*we have seen, we have heard and we have actually handled the Word of Life.*"

While Jesus was on earth, this Levitical Order was functioning and fine-tuned. It held religious and political sway over the people and even over some of the rulers of the Roman Empire. Jesus came as a visitor to that religious order and they never recognized Him. Luke tells us the reason why the city of Jerusalem was going to be destroyed. It was because **"they knew not the time of their visitation."** They had a religious order, a temple, the Holy Place and the Most Holy Place. Everything was working fine, in their opinion. They had all the power, authority and money that they needed and suddenly here came an intruder that was born of and was filled with the Holy Ghost. The record tells us that He performed His miracles by the Holy Ghost. He spoke His words as the Father spoke to Him and taught Him. He was an intruder into their comfortable system. He said, *"I am the temple."* Those were blasphemous words to the religious establishment. Here stood the physical temple of Levi and here stands the Melchizedek temple. Religious hierarchy could not tolerate that. They said this man must go. They even used the Roman government and all of its cruelty to put this man to death because they could not tolerate His competition.

The contrast between the Levitical and the Melchizedek temples is that the Levitical temple was physical and **carnal**. The Melchizedek temple was **living**. He went about doing good: healing the sick, forgiving the sins of the people, bringing them the message of the Almighty. One order was dead while the other was living. Both cannot function at the same time. The Levitical temple order, structure, strength and authority tried to put the Melchizedek to death. The religious machine fiercely guarded that which they thought was the Most Holy Place. *Where was the ark in that Jerusalem temple. It was not there. Where was the mercy seat. It was not there. Where was the glory. It was not there.*

After three and half years of ministry, the disciples who had been with Him and had seen all His wondrous works, were still enthralled with this temple. *"And Jesus went out, and departed from the temple: and his disciples came to him for to shew him the buildings of the temple"* Matthew 24:1. When He went out, the glory went with Him. There was nothing left there but a hollow shell of a building. His disciples came to show Him the buildings of the temple. *"And Jesus said unto them, See ye not all these things? verily I say unto you, There shall not be left here one stone upon another, that shall not be thrown down"* Matthew 24:2. God ordained this temple and He is the one who is going to overthrow it. First the Melchizedek temple has to die on the cross not many days after He makes this statement, but this Temple comes back to life.

When this earthly, carnal, physical Levitical temple is destroyed, it is gone for good. What we see was once God's perfect order of Hebraism turned into Phariseeism or Talmudism-which is still in existence today and which is still opposed to the authority and deity of the Melchizedek Order. When Jesus was in that temple, He told His disciples, *this thing is coming down.* That statement was enough to have Him killed. This Temple, the physical body of our Lord and Savior, in which the Word was made flesh, had to be sacrificed. His blood was sprinkled, not in a physical place in Jerusalem, in a corrupt religious order, but by the Holy Ghost in the heavenly temple in the Heavens. Hebrews 9:14: *"How much more shall the blood of Christ, who through the eternal Spirit offered himself without spot to God ..."*

Observe the contrast between the two temples. Jesus gave His life and was resurrected. He told His disciples it was necessary that He go away, but He had to have a dwelling place yet in the earth. *We are that temple.* Every true child of God, who has been born of the Spirit of God, is of the Melchizedek Order. We are the temple of His body. Ephesians 2:21: *"In whom all the building fitly framed together groweth unto an holy temple in the Lord."* Ephesians 1:23 says: *"Which is his body, the fullness of him that filleth all in all."* His body is the fullness. He is the head. We are members in particular and it is His corporate body that constitutes the fullness of the plan of God.

The Greek word used by Paul in Ephesians is not the one that is referred to when describing the temple in Jerusalem. Paul's word is *'naos'* which means the spiritual temple of God, the same word that is used concerning the body of Jesus Christ when He was on earth. In Ephesians 5:30 it says: *"For we are members of his body, of his flesh, and of his bones."* The writer of this letter is trying to impress on his readers that they are organically connected with Jesus Christ. You are of His body, of His flesh and of His bones. A corporate body refers to the church. Also the present body of the individual believer is the temple of the Holy Ghost. I Corinthians 3:16: *"Know ye not that ye are the temple of God,* [naos] *and that the Spirit of God dwelleth in you.* [He is referring to our physical bodies. *If any man defile the temple of God, him shall God destroy; for the temple of God is holy, which temple ye are."* I Corinthians 6:19 says: *"What? know ye not that your body is the temple of the Holy Ghost which is in you, which ye have of God, and ye are not your own?.* This temple has been purchased with a price; therefore glorify God in your body or in this temple. We have a two-fold responsibility: to glorify God in the spirit and in our physical bodies, which is the true temple of God in the earth.

II Corinthians 6:16 says; *"And what agreement hath the temple of God with idols? for ye are the temple of the living God; as God hath said. I will dwell **in** them, and walk **in** them; and I will be their God, and they shall be my people."* God's temple is no longer a physical building in Jerusalem or a temple made with hands. Even Solomon knew that. Jesus said 'I am with you, but I am going to send another Comforter and He is going to be in you.

When John wrote the Book of Revelation it came to him by revelation. He made several statements such as this one in Revelation 3:12: *"Him that overcometh will I make a pillar in the **temple** of my God, and he shall go no more out: and I will write upon him the name of my God, and the name of the city of my God, which is new Jerusalem, which cometh down out of heaven from my God: and I will write upon him my new name."* Revelation 7:15: *"Therefore are they before the throne of God, and serve him day and night in his **temple**:* [talking about tribulation saints] *and he that sitteth on the throne shall dwell among them.* Revelation 11:19 tells us this: *"And the **temple** of God was opened in heaven, and there was seen in his **temple** the ark of his testament:* [Is this the temple in which Jesus offered His blood?] *and there were lightnings, and voices, and thunderings, and an earthquake, and great hail."* Revelation 14:15, 17: *"And another angel came out of the temple, crying with a loud voice to him that sat on the cloud, Thrust in thy sickle, and reap: for the time is come for thee to reap; for the harvest of the earth is ripe" "And another angel came out of the **temple** which is in heaven, he also having a sharp sickle."* It sounds like a very active temple in the heavens!

Revelation 15:5: *"And after that I looked, and, behold, the **temple** of the tabernacle of the testimony in heaven was opened,.* Revelation 16:1: *"And I heard a great voice out of the **temple** saying to the seven angels, Go your ways, and pour out the vials of the wrath of God upon the earth,....* This heavenly tabernacle has been in existence in the mind of God throughout all eternity. After studying the Scriptures, we can realize that it would be an affront to the Almighty God to gather brick and mortar and build another temple in earthly Jerusalem. Jesus said, "I am the temple," which was offensive to the Pharisees and the leaders of that day. . Now many Christian people are wanting to build a physical temple in Jerusalem and re-establish the rabbinical order once again. That is a double abomination in the sight of Almighty God. Who is the real temple of God. We are that temple, because Jesus is the Head and we are part of His body. **'Naos'** is the Greek word that speaks of the temple of the Holy Spirit. It is not brick and mortar in Jerusalem. No further building **anywhere** is necessary. The Lord has already said you and I are the temple in which He dwells. He is our God and we are His people. He lives and dwells **in** us.

Revelation 21:1-3: *"And I saw a new heaven and a new earth: for the first heaven and the first earth were passed away; and there was no more sea. And I John saw the holy city, new Jerusalem, coming down from God out of heaven, prepared as a bride adorned for her husband. And I heard a great voice out of heaven saying, Behold, the tabernacle of God is with men,* [The dwelling place of the Almighty is with men.] *and he will dwell with them, and they shall be his people, and God himself shall be with them, and be their God."*

Revelation 21:22 says: *"And I saw no* [physical] *temple therein: for the Lord God Almighty and the Lamb are the temple of it."* There is no Levitical temple there. ***Jesus is our temple and we are His temple.*** We dwell in Him. What did Jesus say in John 15. ***"Abide with me."*** You tabernacle in me and I will tabernacle in you. This is strictly a Melchizedek Order relationship.

The Book of Hebrews
Chapter Eight

The Book of Hebrews is one of the most unfathomable books in the Bible. We must go back to the first century in order to understand it. For many years its authorship has been questioned. Possibly in your Bible it says, 'The Epistle of Paul to the Hebrews.' That is not necessarily true. If we go back to the earliest manuscripts the title of this book reads, 'To Hebrews' with no mention of the author. There are several reasons why it was named, 'To Hebrews.' If you take out all the Old Testament references found in the Book of Hebrews, the book would be meaningless. The entire New Testament is based upon the Old Testament, but the Old Testament basis is especially strong in this book.

It was written particularly to people who were familiar with the historical record and the teachings of the Old Testament. The people to whom this book was addressed had to be Israelites, the descendants of Old Testament Israel. If it had been written to non-Israelites, they would have had little or no understanding of what the writer meant with his many Old Testament references. They would know little or nothing about the Old Testament sacrifices, the story of Melchizedek, the high priest and all the other references. The book therefore would be totally meaningless to those readers. So we must keep in mind that in the first century, this book was written to the descendants of Old Testament Israelites.

The book also mentions 'our brother Timothy' in Heb. 13:23. *"Know ye that our brother Timothy is set at liberty; with whom, if he come shortly, I will see you."* Now by this we know that Timothy was still alive at the time. Timothy was a student of the Apostle Paul, and that is why some believe this book was written by the Apostle. Historically, Hebrews is not a late letter, though Timothy could have been older at this time. We do know that possibly Timothy could have been in prison, or this term 'set at liberty' could mean that he had been sent on a mission. Regardless, we know that Timothy was still alive at the time of this writing. It is believed by scholars that this indicates that Hebrews was written sometime between 64 and 68 AD.

THE TITLES OF JESUS

In the Book of Hebrews Jesus Christ is referred to by several different titles. They are as follows: Son, Jesus, Captain of our Salvation, the Apostle and High Priest of our profession, a Priest after the Order of Melchizedek, the Forerunner, the Surety of a Better Testament, a Minister of the Sanctuary, a Mediator of the New Testament, the Author and Finisher of our faith and the Great Shepherd of the Sheep. Those are beautiful titles that we do not find generally elsewhere in the New Testament.

Consider the titles of Jesus. He is the Captain of our salvation. He is the Apostle and the High Priest of our profession of faith. When the writer of Hebrews is making these statements, he is speaking for all of us. So therefore Jesus is the captain of *my* salvation. He is the Apostle and High Priest of *my* profession. The word *'profession'* found in 3:1 means the **terms of our surrender**. It is our confession. He is the **Shepherd** and I am the sheep. I don't lead Him, He leads me. These words also hold the connotation of a covenant. He is the Apostle and High Priest of the covenant that was made, first the Old Covenant and especially the New Covenant. He is the *forerunner* described in 6:20, who has gone into the Most Holy Place in the heavens.

Therefore, since He has gone into the Most Holy Place as a forerunner, and paid the price, we have a right to go into the Most Holy Place, because we have accepted His blood as the perfect sacrifice and covering for our sins. The Bible says, "When *I* see the blood, *I* will pass over you." The blood was applied on the lintel and the door posts of each Hebrew home. His blood is on the lintel and door posts of our heart, our life, our mind; therefore when we approach the door of the Most Holy Place, our one and only qualifying factor is the blood, not our blood, but His blood. The forerunner has entered. How did He enter that Most Holy Place. Hebrews 6:20 tells us: *"Whither the forerunner is for us entered, even Jesus, made an high priest for ever after the order of Melchizedek."* He did not enter that Most Holy Place in the heavens as a Levitical priest. He entered it as a Melchizedek priest. Therefore, we enter it through the merits of the Melchizedek priesthood. Don't try to enter through the Levitical priesthood, it won't work.

THE LIST OF BETTERS

In addition, this is the only book that gives us a list of *'betters.'* Christ is better than the prophets, better than the angels, better than Moses, better than Joshua, better than the High Priest and better than Abraham. We won't find that list anywhere else in the New Testament.

How is Jesus better. *He is stronger in the attributes of His nature, He is mightier in His strength, He is greater in His calling and He is superior in rank*. In other words, they all must bow to Him. What did Joshua say when He saw the LORD. He saw this One coming toward him with His sword drawn. Joshua was captain of the Israelite armies at the time. I am sure Joshua was a little nervous to see this character coming toward him with His sword drawn, just when they were getting ready to attack the city of Jericho. He asked, "Are you for us or against us?. What did the LORD answer. He said, "I have come to take over, I am the captain of the hosts, Joshua. Step aside." The Book of Hebrews tells us that Joshua could not give them rest. Jesus is superior in rank to Joshua and He is much greater in His calling, mightier in His strength, pure and holy in all the attributes of His nature.

It is the only book in the Bible that gives us a second list of '*betters*.' A better hope, a better covenant, better promises, better sacrifices, better substance, a better country, a better resurrection, a better provision and better things than that of Abel. Hebrews 12:24. *"And to Jesus the mediator of the new covenant, and to the blood of sprinkling, that speaketh better things than that of Abel."* This refers to the first sacrifice by Abel recounted in Genesis 4. It should read better things than that of Abel's *offering*. In this verse he is talking about the first offering and the last offering. The first offering took place in the garden of Eden and the last offering took place at Calvary. Other offerings have been made since the offering of Jesus Christ, but every offering for sin after Jesus Christ's death and resurrection is an abomination.

It is the only book that lists the heroes of faith from the Old Testament. It is the only book that uses the phrase, *'by faith'* many times. *By faith* the worlds were framed, Abel offered an excellent sacrifice, Enoch was translated, Noah built the ark, Abraham left Ur of the Chaldees and went into a country unknown to him. It was *by faith* that Sarah received strength to conceive seed, and that Abraham received his son back from the dead. By faith Isaac blessed Jacob and Jacob, when he was dying, blessed the sons of Joseph. It was by faith that their grandfather called those two boys to himself and placed them between his knees and said let my name be named on them. What was his name at that time. Not Jacob, but Jacob/ Israel. 'Let my name be named on those two sons' and we have seen those two sons grow to spread throughout the earth. By faith Joseph, before he died, made mention of the departing of the children of Israel. He said, "take my bones" out of Egypt. We find that beautiful story in a capsule form only in the Book of Hebrews.

Then it says by faith Moses when he was born, was hidden three months. By faith Moses, when he was mature refused to be called the son of Pharaoh's daughter. It was by faith he chose instead to suffer affliction with the people of God rather than to enjoy the pleasures of prosperity in Egypt. By faith they forsook Egypt and kept the Passover. By faith the walls of Jericho fell. By faith the harlot Rahab perished not with them who believed not. Then the writer says, "what more shall I say." Then he lists; Gideon, Barak, Samson, Jephthae, David, Samuel, *"Who through faith subdued kingdoms, wrought righteousness, obtained promises, stopped the mouths of lions, quenched the violence of fire, escaped the edge of the sword, out of weakness were made strong, waxed valiant in fight, turned to flight the armies of the aliens... And these all, having obtained a good report through faith, received not the promise: God having provided some better thing for us, that they without us should not be made perfect.*" (Hebrews 11:33-34, 39-40).

They received not the fulfillment of the promise. God having provided some better thing for whom? For us. He provided a better thing for us. All the people he mentioned above would not be perfected without us. What does that mean. They all died in faith, but they cannot be perfected or come into the full purpose of God because they are waiting for somebody else. For whom are they waiting. They are waiting for us!

In Hebrews 1:1 we read: *"God, who at sundry times and in divers manners spake in time past unto the fathers by the prophets, Hath in these last days* [The last days started at the Day of Pentecost.] *spoken unto us by his Son, whom he hath appointed heir of all things, by whom also he made the worlds;."* Hebrews 12:25: *"See that ye refuse not him that speaketh.* [Who is speaking. The Son, Jesus Christ.] *For if they escaped not who refused him that spake on earth, much more shall not we escape, if we turn away from him that speaketh from heaven:"* In Hebrews 12:21 we find where Moses spoke, trembled and quaked at the experience of Mt. Sinai. The writer of Hebrews tells us, now God is speaking by His Son, Jesus Christ, and the warning is that you must not refuse the voice of the Son. This is not Moses speaking. This is the Son of God. Then the Book of Hebrews gives a warning that no other book in the Bible gives. It gives a warning against *the big temptation.*

The Book of Hebrews begins with Jesus as Creator. Hebrews 1:2-3: *"...Hath in these last days spoken unto us by his Son, whom he hath appointed heir of all things, by whom also he made the worlds; Who being the brightness of his glory, and the express image of his person, and upholding all things by the word of his power, when he had by himself purged our sins, sat down on the right hand of the Majesty on high;"* It starts out mentioning Jesus as **creator,** but it ends in Hebrews 13:20 as Jesus being the **Great Shepherd of the Sheep.** No human mind could come up with such profound thoughts of Jesus Christ being the brightness of the glory of the Almighty and then discuss all of His priesthood through the intervening chapters and end with Jesus being the Great Shepherd of the Sheep. He condescended to our level so that He could shepherd a rebellious and sinful people such as us.

Hebrews 1:. mentions the **death** of Jesus Christ: *"... when he had by himself purged our sins, sat down on the right hand of the Majesty on high;"* He is talking about His sacrifice. It also ends with that same thought in Hebrews 13:20: *"... through the blood of the everlasting covenant,"* The writer of Hebrews being not only inspired, but a gifted orator, a highly educated scholar, with spiritual understanding. He mentions the **resurrection**, both in his introduction and in his closing benediction. He said, *"sat down on the right hand of the Majesty on high;"* in 1:3 and then in 13:20 *"that brought again from the dead our Lord Jesus,"* Basically the same thought. His resurrection and His exaltation are emphasized: *"sat down on the right hand of the Majesty on high;"*

NEW COVENANT CHANGES

Changes are also illustrated in the Book of Hebrews. The administration of death was changed. Let us look at II Corinthians 3:6-10:
*"Who also hath made us able ministers of the new testament; not of
the letter, but of the spirit: for the letter killeth, but the spirit giveth
life. But if the ministration of death, written and engraven in stones,
was glorious,* [This is talking about the first covenant.] *so that the
children of Israel could not steadfastly behold the face of Moses for
the glory of his countenance; which glory was to be done away. How
shall not the ministration of the spirit be rather glorious. For if the
ministration of condemnation* [The law showed us our sins, which
deserves a penalty.] *be glory, much more doth the ministration of
righteousness exceed in glory. For even that which was made glorious had no glory in this respect, by reason of the glory that excelleth."*
The Old Covenant of death or the administration of death had a
glory in it because it was a foreshadowing of a greater covenant
to come. It had no inherent glory, for its only glory portrayed a
future covenant that really contained the glory of righteousness
in it. Its beauty testified of One who is greater, yet who was still
to come. The writer of I Corinthians calls this first covenant the
administration of death.

II Cor. 3:11 tells us. *"For if that which is done away was glorious,*
[the old sacrificial ordinances under the law] *much more that which
remaineth is glorious."* We are living under the Order of Melchizedek
that remains, so it is much more glorious. We are living on this side
of Calvary. In the Old Testament law, they brought their sacrifices
of the blood of bulls and goats, looking forward to a new and

glorious covenant in the future, and we now are living in that new glorious covenant. 'Futurism' says this covenant is going to be made sometime in the future, but the Book of Hebrews tells us that this covenant has already been made with the House of Judah and the House of Israel. Aren't you glad that you are of the House of Judah or the House of Israel. Aren't you glad that you have appropriated the terms of this wonderful profession and covenant, containing the terms of our surrender? Aren't you glad we are living under the terms of the Melchizedek administration and not the Levitical administration?

The old Levitical order became paramount in the minds of the people, so that they could not see the glory of the One who gave it. As we read in Exodus 34:27-35: *"And the LORD said unto Moses, Write thou these words: for after the tenor of these words I have made a covenant with thee and with Israel. And he was there with the LORD forty days and forty nights; he did neither eat bread, nor drink water. And he wrote upon the tables the words of the covenant, the ten commandments. And it came to pass, when Moses came down from mount Sinai with the two tables of testimony in Moses' hand, when he came down from the mount, that Moses knew not that the skin of his face shone while he talked with him. And when Aaron and all the children of Israel saw Moses, behold, the skin of his face shone; and they were afraid to come nigh him. And Moses called unto them; and Aaron and all the rulers of the congregation returned unto him: and Moses talked with them. And afterward all the children of Israel came nigh: and he gave them in commandment all that the LORD had spoken with him in mount Sinai. And till Moses had done speaking with them, he put a veil on his face. But when Moses went in before*

*the LORD to speak with him, he took the veil off, until he came out.
And he came out, and spake unto the children of Israel that which
he was commanded. And the children of Israel saw the face of Moses,
that the skin of Moses' face shone: and Moses put the veil upon his
face again, until he went in to speak with him."*

The people told Moses; 'we don't like this Sinai experience where
the mountain quakes. You talk to God and tell us what God says,
but don't let God speak to us directly.' The veil that was over Moses'
face, kept them from seeing the glory of God. They didn't want to
see the glory of God on Moses' face. Sinful man doesn't want to
see the glory of God. They want to see a veil between them and the
glory. But there are people who want the veil removed. We want
to see the glory of God. We hear and read His words, but we want
to see Him in the fullness of His glory. Moses experienced that
shining face which was a foreshadow of what would happen on
the Mount of Transfiguration. There on that mountain the whole
body of Jesus shone as the glory of God filled His own body and
His disciples even saw it.

The veil over the face of Moses represented the spiritual barrier
between the people and God. Later, the veil in the temple was
a spiritual barrier between the people and the presence of God.
When Jesus died the veil was rent from top to the bottom, signifying that the way into the Most Holy Place is now complete. Jesus
as the forerunner went in, but not into that place in Jerusalem, but
into the one in the heavens. You have a right to enter into the Most
Holy Place. That veil is no longer the barrier. The writer of Hebrews
actually tells us, the veil that was broken was His flesh.

Another thing was changed in the Book of Hebrews. Enmity came about between the two houses, Israel and Judah, because of their self righteousness in following the law of dogmatic ordinances. He is our peace, says Ephesians 2:14. Israel and Judah were brought back together in peace. Some people look forward to that occurring strictly in the future. I look forward to it being materialized and brought into its greater fulfillment, but it was already completed on the cross. He is our peace. The Levitical priesthood brought enmity, but the Melchizedek priesthood brought peace.

Another change in the Book of Hebrews we find in chapter 4. Verse 1: "*Let us therefore fear, lest, a promise being left us of entering into his rest,* [based on the words of chapter 3] *any of you should seem to come short of it. For unto us was the gospel preached, as well as unto them: but the word preached did not profit them* [the Israelites in the Old Testament] *not being mixed with faith in them that heard it. For we which have believed do enter into rest, as he said, As I have sworn in my wrath, if they shall enter into my rest: although the works were finished from the foundation of the world. For he spake in a certain place of the seventh day on this wise, And God did rest the seventh day from all his works. And in this place again, If they shall enter into my rest. Seeing therefore it remaineth that some must enter therein, and they to whom it was first preached entered not in because of unbelief: Again, he limiteth a certain day, saying in David, To day, after so long a time; as it is said, To day if ye will hear his voice, harden not your hearts. For if Jesus* [Joshua] *had given them rest, then would he not afterward have spoken of another day.* [Then he gives us this climactic thought. *There remaineth therefore a rest to the people of God. For he that is entered into his rest, he also hath ceased from his own works, as God did from his.*"

The writer compares spiritual rest to the seventh day. God set up in His creation activities in a cycle and established the seventh day. Then the record says He rested from all His works. God has not done away with the seventh day. That is not what the writer of Hebrews is telling us. Man's physical body needs that Sabbath day cycle. **Sabbath means rest.** It does not mean worship, it means rest. The Sabbath is *time* that God has given us in the seven-day cycle specifically set aside to rest. Our society needs the seven-day cycle.

Pharisees exercised their greatest hypocrisy in their expression of the observance of the Sabbath. 'How dare you heal that man on the Sabbath,' in rebuking Jesus. Here was the Lord of Glory who made the Sabbath and they were dictating its observance to Him. It was the apex of hypocrisy. Sabbath-keeping among the Pharisees and the Scribes was the absolute pinnacle of their self-righteousness. The Book of Hebrews says they had no rest. Worshiping on Saturday or on Sunday should not be bondage. The true Sabbath is our rest in Christ. The seventh day is the expression of God's creation work and of His control over the entire universe and should be the expression of His control in an Israelite civilization. They were angry when Jesus healed a lame man on the Sabbath when He is the One Who made the Sabbath. What religious bondage! They would not defile their concept of the Sabbath day by allowing the healing of one in need, but they were willing to crucify the One who made the Sabbath. That is religious hypocrisy. Denominationalism can become bondage if the leaders emphasize one or two points of doctrine to control the people by them. The Israelite people did not have rest under Joshua. They invaded the Promised Land, took it over and still did not have rest. Hebrews four tells us that we wait for another day, because, "*There remaineth therefore a rest to the people of God.*"

Rejection of the Melchizedek Priesthood
Chapter Nine

The role and meaning of the Melchizedek Priesthood is a foundational subject in the Bible. It is such a vast concept that it becomes an integral part of the crucifixion of Jesus Christ, a vital inflow into prophecy and weaves itself into history. It impacts many events and ideas.

Jesus Christ is God's means of divine revelation throughout history, particularly in its final days. The 'last days' began during the first century A.D. The Apostle Peter said that he was living in the last days and Paul said they were living in the last days. We are given a warning in Hebrews 12:25: *"See that ye refuse not him that speaketh. For if they escaped not who refused him that spake on earth, much more shall not we escape, if we turn away from him that speaketh from heaven:"* That is telling us that some people heard Jesus Christ in the flesh and they refused Him. He is now speaking to us by His Spirit and the writer says 'be cautious, don't refuse Him who is now speaking by the Holy Spirit.' Then he adds another thought, he says, *'much more,'* giving the impression that we are more responsible today, we who are supposed to be listening to Him by the Holy Spirit within us, than were those who heard Him only in the flesh. He says, *"much more shall not we escape, if we turn away from him that speaketh from heaven:"* This is a serious matter about which the Book of Hebrews gives a warning. ***Don't refuse Him that speaks from heaven.***

This second serious warning is found in chapters six and ten. This was ***the big temptation*** of the first century Christians. Now transport your mind over nineteen hundred years and put yourself in the place of those first century Hebrew Christians. Use your imagination and seat yourself in a congregation, most likely meeting in a home. Some older people who remembered the ministry of Jesus Christ (which took place from 27-31 AD) also recalled the Levitical priesthood, with all the offerings they had to bring to the temple, all the legalities that were involved in obeying the law, and the condemnation of the High Priest. They saw Jesus and remembered how the rumors went wild when He claimed to be the Son of God and claimed to forgive sins. Those were the two blasphemies recognized by the Jewish hierarchy. These saints remembered the crucifixion and how they were on edge for three days because this Man said He was going to overcome death. He said, 'You destroy this temple and in three days I am going to raise it up.' Before He was crucified He had to go through six trials, three religious and three civil. He was tried in the palace of the High Priest. He was condemned by the other priests. They hired false witnesses against Him and then He was taken to Pilate. From there He was taken to Herod and then was sent back to Pilate, going through six different trials. Their verdict was predetermined. They hated Him from the beginning, because He had exposed the falseness of the religious hierarchy of the day and had said things like, 'See that sepulcher over there, see how it is washed and white on the outside, the pretense is beautiful, but inside it is full of dead men's bones. You are the same way.'

Jesus looked at the Pharisees one day and said, "Ye are of your father the devil." Not a very popular thing to say. He was exposing the hypocrisy, corruption and the perversion of the Levitical priesthood that He had given in its purity to the Hebrew people in the beginning. Man corrupted the Levitical priesthood, not God. God made it as a temporary thing until the Melchizedek Order would come into force, yet man corrupted it to such an extent that it actually became an enemy of God. God had no choice but to destroy it because of its stench of evil.

Now Jesus was risen and had ascended to Heaven. Christians met together for encouragement and worship. They were gathered together remembering all the things in Jesus' ministry. But another fear has settled on this small New Testament, first century congregation. The Roman government was filled with threats and treachery. They began to hear about a man named Nero who had not yet ascended to the throne, but they understood that he was vicious. They were hoping that he would not assume the office of the highest position in the land, yet he did. That was the political threat, for the Roman Empire had said that Christians were a threat to its existence. They claimed that Christians were atheists because they refused to worship Caesar. No doubt a younger person would look at an older one and say, 'What do you mean we are atheists. We are anything but atheists.' The definition by the Roman Empire of an 'atheist' was as follows: *anyone who would not say that Caesar was not only king but God. 'Atheists' would not recognize the state as supreme.*

What is the greatest threat and the *greatest temptation* mentioned in the Book of Hebrews. It is not the Roman government. It is not civil authorities. It is Phariseeism, the Jewish hierarchy. That is the subject of the warning in the Book of Hebrews. The writer of the Book of Hebrews never even mentions the political threat to

Christians in the first century. He mentions only the temptation to go back to Phariseeism, which today is known as Judaism. When we read the Book of Acts, the religious order took these Christians before the civil authorities. The civil authorities did not go after Christians on their own. The religious authority, the Pharisees, the scribes, the chief priests and elders were vehemently revengeful in their attack against New Testament Christians. The most outstanding example was the life of Saul before he became the apostle Paul. In Acts 9:1 it says: *"And Saul, yet breathing out threatenings and slaughter against the disciples of the Lord, went unto the high priest,"* Against who? Against the Christians, but where did he receive his authority. Not from the civil authorities, but from the religious government, the chief priests, the elders and the scribes.

First century Christians were therefore justifiably filled with fear, for they were threatened by the government on one side and the religious leaders on the other. But there was a way out. If they would just compromise and go back into Judaism, everything would be all right. The threat would wane and disappear. Then Paul was converted and they became suspicious of him. His experience and education made him a driving force in the growth of Christianity, yet he faced this same temptation, because the Judaizers followed him around, saying to the people, "yes, you are saved by grace, BUT you need to be circumcised. You have to be saved both by grace and by circumcision and that is your true means of salvation." Finally they succeeded in getting the civil authorities to cut Paul's head off. These Christians to whom this letter was addressed had the same threat leveled against them as did the Apostle Paul. If they would just compromise with the

Pharisees and go back under the Levitical order, the threat to their lives would be lessened. ***This was the big temptation***.

Turning to the Book of Titus 1:10-14, we see evidence of this: *"For there are many unruly and vain talkers and deceivers, specially they of the circumcision: Whose mouths must be stopped, who subvert whole houses, teaching things which they ought not, for filthy lucre's sake. One of themselves, even a prophet of their own, said, The Cretans are always liars, evil beasts, slow bellies.* [idle and lazy] *This witness is true. Wherefore rebuke them sharply, that they may be sound in the faith; Not giving heed to Jewish fables,* [not Roman fables] *and commandments of men, that turn from the truth. "They profess that they know God; but in* works *they deny him, being abominable, and disobedient, and unto every good work reprobate."*

HISTORICAL BACKGROUND

This historical era can be traced back to the Old Testament. Daniel 8:1-13: *"In the third year of the reign of King Belshazzar a vision appeared unto me, even unto me Daniel, after that which appeared unto me at the first. And I saw in a vision; and it came to pass, when I saw, that I was at Shushan* [Babylon] *in the palace, which is in the province of Elam; and I saw in a vision, and I was by the river of Ulai. Then I lifted up mine eyes, and saw, and, behold, there stood before the river a ram which had two horns: and the two horns were high; but one was higher than the other, and the higher came up last. I saw the ram pushing westward, and northward, and southward; so that no beasts might stand before him. neither was there any that could deliver out of his hand; but he did according to his will, and became great.* [This is speaking of the dual kingdom of the Medes and the Persians. This is a chronological explanation of these kingdoms because one horn became greater than the other.] *And as I was considering, behold, an he goat came from the west on the face of the whole earth, and touched not the ground: and the goat had a notable horn between his eyes. And he came to the ram that had two horns, which I had seen standing before the river, and ran unto him in the fury of his power. And I saw him come close unto the ram, and he was moved with choler against him, and smote the ram, and brake his two horns: and there was no power in the ram to stand before him, but he cast him down to the ground, and stamped upon him: and there was none that could deliver the ram out of his hand".*

This he goat was Alexander the Great, who came from the west, which at one time was known as Macedonia. He was the leader of the Grecian Empire, but actually he was a Macedonian. It says in verse 8: *"Therefore the he goat waxed very great: and when he was strong, the great horn was broken;* [Alexander the Great died at the apex of his career at the age of 33.] *and for it came up four notable ones* [his four generals who took over] *toward the four winds of heaven. And out of one of them came forth a little horn, which waxed exceeding great,* [The Roman Empire, which had not actually become an empire at this time.] *toward the south, and toward the east, and toward the pleasant land.* [Palestine] *And it waxed great, even to the host of heaven; and it cast down some of the host and of the stars to the ground, and stamped upon them.* [The hosts of heaven would be the Levitical hierarchy, the priests, the scribes, elders etc., in the land of Judah.] *Yea, he magnified himself even to the prince of the host, and by him the daily sacrifice was taken away, and the place of his sanctuary was cast down.*

And an host was given him against the daily sacrifice by reason of transgression, and it cast down the truth to the ground; and it practiced, and prospered. Then I heard one saint speaking, and another saint said unto that certain saint which spake, How long shall be the vision concerning the daily sacrifice, and the transgression of desolation, to give both the sanctuary and the host to be trodden under foot?" The sanctuary was the Temple of Solomon and the host was the Levitical hierarchy of that day. Both of them were going to be destroyed by this one of the Roman Empire whose name was Titus Flavius.

Daniel begins with the Medo-Persian Empire. Then Alexander the Great came along and fell at the peak of his greatness and his four generals took over. The Roman government was then formed. The Roman city/state and the Roman Empire were the force historically that brought an end to the daily sacrifice in 70 AD. It was preordained that Titus the Roman General surround the city of Jerusalem. They quarantined that place and people died by the thousands. It mentioned the words **transgression of desolation** in Daniel 9:26-27: *"And after threescore and two weeks shall Messiah be cut off, but not for himself: and the people of the prince* [the Romans of Titus the prince] *that shall come shall destroy the city and the sanctuary; and the end thereof shall be with a flood, and unto the end of the war desolations are determined. And he shall confirm the covenant with many for one week:* [That is the Messiah.] *and in the midst of the week he shall cause the sacrifice and the oblation to cease, and for the overspreading of abominations he shall make it desolate, even until the consummation, and that determined shall be poured upon the desolate."*

Here is the crux of the matter. The Jewish hierarchy of that day despised the sacrifice of Jesus Christ. It was preordained and prophesied here that one of the purposes of the coming of the Messiah was to bring an end to the daily sacrifices. He alone is the supreme sacrifice for sin, once and for all. But the hierarchy did not stop the sacrifices, they continued. The historian Josephus tells us that they still continued the daily sacrifices until the final destruction of the temple in 70 AD. In verse 27 we see that Messiah *"shall cause the sacrifice and the oblation to cease, and for the overspreading of abominations he shall make it desolate, even until the consummation, and that determined shall be poured upon the desolate."* The word abomination means an act whereby a pagan idol is introduced into the precincts of the holy temple in Jerusalem. ***This unholy idol is any animal sacrifice for sin after the perfect sacrifice was made.*** That is an abomination. The sacrifice is an idol and God says that He will destroy the temple in Jerusalem. At the precise time during the Roman Empire when Titus was in charge, He would destroy the temple, the city and bring the Levitical sacrifice to an end. That sacrifice was false, reprehensible and despicable.

The church world does not put emphasis on this interpretation. In fact sometimes the teaching is totally opposite. This is what is in the original manuscripts: ***"In the temple of the Lord there shall be an abomination."*** The Latin Vulgate translation says, *"In the temple there shall be an abomination."* The Septuagint says, *"And upon the temple there shall be an abomination of desolation."* Where is this abomination going to be? In the temple.

Daniel 11:31: *"And arms* [Romans] *shall stand on his part, and they shall pollute the sanctuary of strength,* [the fortified temple at Jerusalem] *and shall take away the daily sacrifice, and they shall place the abomination that maketh desolate.* When we think of the temple in Jerusalem, don't think of just a little church house. This was a massive structure, containing living quarters and towers for defense. They were made with double and triple walls for protection. This 'building' was a small city in itself.

Some prophecy preachers say this prophecy has already taken place, but does not apply to 70 AD, while others say it is yet to come in the future. Those who go further back beyond 70 AD say that this abomination of desolation or false sacrifice in the temple took place when the Syrian king, Antiochus Epiphanes, forced the people to sacrifice a pig on the altar around 65 BC. He captured Jerusalem and stayed there for three and a half years. That was an abomination. Mohammed committed sacrilege there around 625 AD when he sacrificed a pig on the Jewish altar. The 'futurists' say that this will be fulfilled when the antichrist sits in the temple in the city of Jerusalem. This same antichrist figure was a historical person who keeps changing, such as Hitler, Mussolini, FDR or others. But when each alleged antichrist died off, the futurists needed to find another. If we read the whole Bible in its proper context, we find that Jesus Christ and His sacrifice of Calvary is the pivotal point of history and not some antichrist. We will then understand the definition of the abomination of desolation. *It is the rejection of the pure and holy sacrifice of Jesus Christ upon Calvary and this rejection will result in desolation and destruction.* We know there are those among us today who still despise the sacrifice of Jesus Christ with utter contempt. God will deal with them.

Keep in mind the same phrase, the abomination of desolation or
the abomination that worketh desolation which results in destruction. In Matthew 24:15 we read the words of Jesus Christ Himself,
putting the subject into the proper 70 AD context. Some people
believe this abomination is yet future, but it has already taken place:
*"When ye therefore shall see the abomination of desolation, spoken
of by Daniel the prophet, stand in the holy place, (whoso readeth, let
him understand:)* [Daniel said the wise shall understand] *Then let
them which be in Judaea flee into the mountains: Let him which is
on the housetop not come down to take any thing out of his house:
Neither let him which is in the field return back to take his clothes.
And woe unto them that are with child, and to them that give suck in
those days! But pray ye that your flight be not in the winter, neither
on the sabbath day:"*

This prophecy was given in Jeremiah 6:1 to the Benjamites, warning
them to flee the city. This is also the warning Jesus personally gave
to the disciples who were Benjamites. They were at the temple and
the disciples said to Him, 'Look at this magnificent temple' and He
turned around and said, 'Yes, it is magnificent, but not one stone
will be left upon another.' Then He warns them, 'get out now before
the desolation takes place because when you see the abomination
taking place in the temple, then I am going to bring desolation to
this place.' He prophesied that in 31 AD. Forty years later God had
had enough. Luke 19:41: *"And when he was come near, he beheld
the city, and wept over it, Saying, If thou hadst known, even thou,
at least in this thy day, the things which belong unto thy peace! but
now they are hid from thine eyes. For the days shall come upon thee,
that thine enemies shall cast a trench about thee, and compass thee*

round, and keep thee in on every side, And shall lay thee even with the ground, and thy children within thee; and they shall not leave in thee one stone upon another; because thou knewest not the time of thy visitation." **They knew not the time of their visitation and did not recognize that Jesus was the visitor.**

In Luke 23:27-31 Jesus uttered a warning when He was bearing His cross to Calvary: *"And there followed him a great company of people, and of women, which also bewailed and lamented him. But Jesus turning unto them said, Daughters of Jerusalem, weep not for me, but weep for yourselves, and for your children. For, behold, the days are coming, in the which they shall say, Blessed are the barren, and the wombs that never bare, and the paps which never gave suck. Then shall they begin to say to the mountains, Fall on us; and to the hills, Cover us. For if they do these things in a green tree, what shall be done in the dry?.* These are warnings of Jesus to that generation because the Pharisees had rejected Him. This is not a popular interpretation, but this is the interpretation of our forefathers. It is the approach that Bible scholars believed until the 'rapture theory' came along.

THE TESTIMONY OF JOSEPHUS

In 70 AD during the seize of Jerusalem, Josephus, the great Jewish historian recorded: "The sacrifice called the daily sacrifice had failed. It had not been offered to God for want of men to offer it." This tells us that they were still offering the sacrifice in 70 AD. He then goes on to record that God gave the people five different supernatural warnings of the destruction to come:

Number one - A star resembling a sword stood over the city and a comet continued or lasted for a whole year. This was before 70 AD. Remember the city was besieged for three years and people were dying all over the city.

Number two - "Before the Jews' rebellion and before the commotions that preceded the war, when the people were coming in great crowds for the Feast of Unleavened Bread, on the eighth day of the month, Nisan, and at the ninth hour of the night [three AM] so great a light shown round about the altar and the holy house that it appeared to be bright daytime which light lasted a half hour. This light seemed to be a good sign to the unlearned, but was interpreted by the sacred scribes as to portend those events which immediately followed."

Number three - The sacrificial ritual was proceeding. Then came the third sign. "At the same festival also, as this heifer was led by the high priest to the altar to be sacrificed, brought forth a lamb in the midst of the temple."

Number four - "Moreover the Eastern gate of the temple which was of brass and vastly heavy and had been with difficulty shut by twenty men and rested upon bases armed with iron and had bolts fastened very deep in the firm floor which was there made of one entire stone. [This huge gate] was seen to be opened on its own accord about the sixth hour of the night. [Was this like the release of Peter from prison. The story in the Book of Acts tells us that the gates opened on their own.] Now those who kept watch in the temple came here upon running to the captain of the temple and told him of it who then came up thither and not without great difficulty was able to shut the gate again. Now to those that were unlearned they thought it was a good sign but to the men of learning, the security of their holy house was dissolved of its own accord and the gate was opened for the advantage of the enemies."

Number five - "There was a man by the name of Jesus, He prophesied against the temple for four years. He was a husbandman [farmer] who four years before the war began and at the time when the city was at great peace and prosperity came to the Feast whereon it is our custom to make Tabernacles to God in the temple, began to cry suddenly. "A voice from the east, a voice from the west, a voice from the four winds, a voice against Jerusalem and the holy house. A voice against the bridegrooms and the brides and a voice against this whole people." This was his cry as he went about by day and night in all the lanes of the city. Certain of the most eminent among the populace had great indignation at this dire cry of his and took up the man and gave him a great number of severe stripes, yet did not he either say anything for himself or anything peculiar for those who chastised him but still he went on with the same words. Hereupon our rulers supposing as the case proved to be that this was a sort of divine fury in the man, brought him to the procurator where he was whipped until his bones were laid bare yet he did not make any supplication for himself or shed his tears but turning his voice to the most lamentable tone possible at every stroke of the whip his answer was "Woe, woe to Jerusalem." God sent that man as a witness against the city of Jerusalem and his cry when he was being whipped was; woe, woe to Jerusalem.

What took place during this siege. Josephus tells us this: Factions inside the city fought against one another. It wasn't just the Roman army on the outside. Rebels were going around within the city creating chaos and mayhem. They were fighting one another for control of the city and they would not give up. Titus gave them chances to give up. He had spokesmen and even had Josephus himself speak to the Jewish leaders of the city of Jerusalem. They would not give up, because these rebels were in charge. They were robbers, murderers and the base elements of society. They went about killing many priests as they performed their sacred administrations. They were merciless. They were also looking for food like everybody else. One faction had 10,000 men. We must remember that the city of Jerusalem was a very big city. The number of casualties was actually 1,100,000 who died by the hands of the Romans, by starvation and by the hands of one another. Neighbors were killing neighbors for a morsel of bread or wheat and there were over 97,000 people who were taken captive by the Romans.

When Jesus Christ said there was coming a desolation that is exactly what He meant. He said not one stone would be left upon another. As we all know the city was attacked by the Roman army, the buildings burned, the rocks were separated, and the gold was taken with the precious stones and metals from the instruments that were at one time used for sacred purposes. Jesus said to the women as He walked on Calvary's road, 'Don't weep for me, weep for yourself and for your children.' People were starving to death. They would eat anything. The robbers would chew on the leather of their belts. They actually started to eat one another. When a relative died they did not always bury their body. They ate that body. Mothers actually ate their babies.

One account says: "In so much that children pulled the very morsels that their fathers were eating out of their very mouths. What was still more to be pitied was what the mothers did to their infants. When those that were dear were perishing under their hands they were not ashamed to take from them the very last drop that might preserve their lives. While they ate after this manner, yet were they not concealed in so doing. But seditious [individuals] everywhere came upon them immediately and snatched away from them what they had gotten from others. For when they saw any house shut up, this was a signal to them that the house within had gotten some food. Whereupon they opened the doors, ran in and took pieces of what they were eating, almost out of their very throats, and this by force. The old men that held their food fast were beaten and if the women hid what they had within their hands, their hair was torn for so doing. Neither was there any commiseration shown to the aged or the infant. They lifted up children from the ground as they hung upon the morsels they had gotten and shook them down upon the floor, but still were they more barbarously cruel to those who had prevented their coming in and had actually swallowed down what they were going to seize upon and if they had been unjustly defrauded of their right they also invented terrible methods of torment to discover any food. To shut up the passages of the privy parts of the miserable wretches and to drive sharp stakes up their fundament. A man was forced to bear what is even terrible to hear in order to make him confess that he had only one loaf of bread or that he might discover a handful of barley meal that was concealed." If they knew someone had just swallowed food, they would get it out of their body and eat it themselves.

A WARNING TO SAINTS

When Jesus said there was a desolation coming that is just what He meant. People resorted to eating dung. People ate their own children. There were so many people dead in the streets, when these different rebellious factions were fighting one another they were actually walking on dead bodies. There were not enough healthy men to bury the dead. Some of them who were attempting to bury the dead, fell dead from starvation while they were burying others. Now Jesus had predicted in Matthew 24 that this was coming to pass. He told His disciples to get out now. He knew what was coming.

The writer of Hebrews is writing to these saints and giving them a warning which was written before 70 AD. We read Hebrews 12:25 and the warning was: 'Do not refuse to hear the Son of God speak from heaven.' Hebrews 12:26 is a prophecy concerning the destruction of Jerusalem: "*Whose voice then shook the earth: but now he hath promised, saying, Yet once more I shake not the earth only, but also heaven.*" It doesn't mean that the sun itself will be shaken, or the moon and the stars. He is talking about religious governments. Verse 27. "*And this word, Yet once more, signifieth the removing of those things that are shaken, as of things that are made, that those things which cannot be shaken may remain. Wherefore we receiving a kingdom which cannot be moved,* [He is talking to these saints, saying don't go back to Judaism because four years from now everything that can be shaken will be shaken, but we have a kingdom that cannot be shaken. Hold on, Saints] *let us have grace, whereby we may serve God acceptably with reverence and godly fear:* [Why?] *For our God is a consuming fire.*

Hebrews 6:4-6. *"For it is impossible for those who were once enlight-ened,* [He is talking to the Hebrew saints.] *and have tasted of the heavenly gift, and were made partakers of the Holy Ghost, And have tasted the good word of God, and the powers of the world to come, If they shall fall away,* [apostatize or return back to Judaism] *to renew them again unto repentance; seeing they crucify to themselves the Son of God afresh, and put him to an open shame."* **What is an open shame. It is to officially proclaim Jesus an imposter and worthy of death.** The writer says they put Him to an open shame, as they continued to have the sacrifices in Jerusalem; they deemed Him an imposter because they did not accept His sacrifice and therefore thought Him worthy of death. Rejecting Him is an abomination and there is no more repentance.

In verses 7-9, the author gives an illustration of the earth taking in the rain: *"For the earth which drinketh in the rain that cometh oft upon it, and bringeth forth herbs meet for them by whom it is dressed, receiveth blessing from God: But that which beareth thorns and briers is rejected, and is nigh unto cursing; whose end is to be burned. But, beloved, we are persuaded better things of you, and things that accompany salvation, though we thus speak."* What are the thorns and briars. Saints who take in the rain and bring forth only briars and thorns. In other words, they return to Judaism, and are rejected, nigh unto cursing whose end is to be burned.

Heb. 10:26, *"For if we sin willfully after that we have received the knowledge of the truth, there remaineth no more sacrifice for sins,"* Some may teach if a Christian tells a little fib, he is lost forever. If you sin at all you are bound for hell. That is not what this verse means.

He is telling these Hebrews, if you willingly turn back to animal sacrifice. Judaism or Phariseeism, there is no more sacrifice. You are lost. Going on to verse 27; *"But a certain fearful looking for of judgment and fiery indignation, which shall devour the adversaries. He that despised Moses' law died without mercy under two or three witnesses: Of how much sorer punishment, suppose ye, shall he be thought worthy, who hath trodden under foot the Son of God, and hath counted the blood of the covenant, wherewith he was sanctified, an unholy thing, and hath done despite* [**insult**] *unto the Spirit of grace?"* [This word unholy in this case means '**of no value**.'] *"For we know him that hath said, Vengeance belongeth unto me, I will recompense, saith the Lord. And again, The Lord shall judge his people. It is a fearful thing to fall into the hands of the living God."*

What is the abomination of desolation? It was committed by an old Order and by a people who propagated that Order. It was a religion that rejected the sacrifice of Jesus and continued their animal sacrifices, thereby deeming His blood of no value. This rejection put Him to an open shame. They considered Him an imposter. Here is the King of Glory making the Melchizedek sacrifice once and for all and the Levitical Order raises its ugly head in its perverted state, saying in effect; 'We despise You and Your sacrifice. We will not accept the Melchizedek priesthood. We will crucify You because we deem You an absolute devil, an imposter and Your blood is valueless. It is unholy and we have the courage to cry, 'Your blood be on us and our children.' This is also called the blasphemy against the Holy Ghost. It is not committed by an individual; it was committed by a corporate people. God have mercy on those people. They are still among us and they still consider His blood of no value.

False Religion Confronts Melchizedek
Chapter 10

Matthew 21 to 24 are four consecutive chapters detailing a face-to-face confrontation of our Lord with the religious leaders of His day. A big percentage of the Book of Matthew is written from the standpoint of our Lord's doctrines that irritated those leaders, while the poor and common people heard Him gladly. This power structure held the people in bondage. Nothing appears to have changed to this day.

In Matthew 22:15-40 we find three groups of people who are asking Jesus questions. Each group had a different question and each one was influenced by a somewhat different standpoint. The three different groups were the Herodians, the Pharisees and the Sadducees. They didn't necessarily like one another, but they were united against a common enemy and that was the Lord Jesus Christ. Keep in mind that this occurs just before the warning that Jesus gives concerning the Temple in Matthew 24. After that came His arrest, six trials and crucifixion. So this is at the very end of His ministry.

The Herodians were coming from the standpoint of **legality**. The Sadducees were coming from a hypothetical **doctrinal** standpoint, and the Pharisees from a **religious** standpoint of trying to test His allegiance to what they considered the unchanging nature of God.

THE HERODIANS

Notice that the Pharisees are mentioned in conjunction with the Herodians. The Pharisees were the instigators of all this turmoil. They were the ones behind the scenes who contrived all the conspiracies, intrigue and the questions whereby they would attempt to trick our Savior. They would use anybody to do their dirty work, friend or foe. Nothing has changed to this day. We read in Matthew 22:15: *"Then went the Pharisees, and took counsel how they might entangle him in his talk. And they sent out unto him their disciples with the Herodians ..."* Do you get the picture. They took counsel, no doubt secret counsel. The Pharisees, the bigwigs, were talking, saying, 'How can we trap Him. Things were heating up in Jerusalem because Jesus had declared Himself to be the Son of God. He has already had His triumphal entry into Jerusalem and the people hailed Him the Son of David. Their counsel would have been something like this. 'We cannot have this man go any further, we must put Him to silence. Who can we use to approach Him. We have directly approached Him many times before. Can we get another influential group to do our dirty work. Yes, let's try the Herodians this time.'

The Herodians were a group who were associated with the fortunes of the Herodian family. This was a very powerful family in politics, who believed in the doctrines of Herod. The doctrines of Herod are not spelled out plainly in the Bible, but we know that the **leaven of Herod** is referred to by our Savior. Leaven was representative of Herod's doctrine or what he taught. He wielded persuasive power over people to win their allegiance back to him. This does not refer to the Herod in Rome. This is the Herod, the governor of Galilee. Herod the Great was ruling at the time Jesus was born and died a little after Jesus was born, possibly two years later. His father, Herod Antipater, was a man who came up through the ranks of government in Judaea and Palestine, after the Hasmonian Jewish element conquered Edom. They went into Idumea around 125 BC and conquered the land of Edom. Herod Antipater was an Edomite. John Hyrcanus, that Jewish zealot, was so powerful in his military conquest that he forced the Edomites to accept Judaism even to the point of circumcision.

Therefore Herod, the grandfather of the Herod who was ruling when Jesus was crucified, was an Edomite from the land of Idumea. That land is south and east of Jerusalem, on the east side of the Jordan River near the Dead Sea. The Edomites had been the perpetual enemies of the people of God. They had accepted Judaism or Talmudism by force. Antipater became very powerful in government because the Jews had conquered them, but Rome had conquered Palestine. They were subjects of Rome, and Herod Antipater grew up under Roman government, but in the Jewish religion. He considered himself Jewish, as did the whole Herod family, because they had adopted the Jewish religion on the authority of the Pharisees.

Herod the Great was an Edomite, the son of an Arabian woman and a member of the Jewish religion. When Jesus was born Herod figured that this one, who was called the "King of the Jews," was going to be a threat to him, so therefore he must get rid of Him. We know the story of the slaughter of all the boys two years old and under in the region surrounding Bethlehem. Herod the Great, [who died shortly after the birth of Jesus Christ] also rebuilt the temple which took him 46 years to finish. Why did he rebuild the temple. He was a member of their religion, but he was an Edomite by heredity. He was very friendly with the Jewish people and was therefore influential in Rome for the benefit of the Jews in Palestine. Building the temple in Jerusalem was only one part of all the many public works that Herod did while he was on the throne. He became very powerful because he was a friend to the Jewish people and had their allegiance. He had religious and political power and saw a threat from this Child who was born, "King of the Jews."

Herod Antipas took the throne after his father. For a period of time he had the allegiance of the people, but he was a ruthless man. These men in power were not Romans; they were really not Jewish. They were Edomites who had adopted the Jewish religion and were playing the political cards between the Jews and Rome. They needed to maintain favor with Caesar. Caesar had the authority to banish them and that is what eventually happened to this man. He is the man who married Herodias, the wife of his half brother, Philip. Herodias was a vile woman and was reproved by a man of God, John the Baptist. Herod killed John the Baptist approximately three and half years before the events recorded in Matthew 22, so this political debacle that Herod Antipas had committed was still a topic of interest. Many people loved John the Baptist, so therefore Herod fell out of favor with a lot of the people after John's death.

A political and a religious power struggle was going on. These Pharisees wanted to maintain the **religious** upper hand and the Herodians wanted to keep the **political** upper hand. This man Jesus Christ was a threat to both of them. He is still a threat. Politicians don't like Him. They will use His name for clout, but they really don't like Him and especially when you tell them about the law of God. The religious leaders cannot tolerate Him. It is fortunate for them that Jesus lived two thousand years ago and He is basically out of their hair.

In order to entangle Jesus in His teaching, consider this question that they asked Him. Verse 16: *"And they sent out unto him their disciples with the Herodians, saying, Master, we know that thou art true, and teachest the way of God in truth, neither carest thou for any man: for thou regardest not the person of men."* That is what you call flattery. Verse 17: *"Tell us therefore, What thinkest thou? Is it lawful to give tribute unto Caesar, or not?.* Here the Herodians were asking Him a question of legality. Pilate was on the throne and he was a Roman, not an Edomite. They were going to try to get Jesus in trouble with Pilate who would send a courier to Rome. Rome would send somebody to Palestine to take care of this man Jesus. They were actually hoping that Jesus would answer, "No, it is not good, it is not proper or lawful to give tribute to Caesar." That way they would have tricked Him.

Verse 18: *"But Jesus perceived their wickedness, and said, Why tempt ye me, ye hypocrites?"* Jesus knew that the question was simply a means of tripping Him up and He answered in verse 19-21: *"Shew me the tribute money. And they brought unto him a penny. And he saith unto them, Whose is this image and superscription? They say unto him, Caesar's. Then saith he unto them, Render therefore unto Caesar the things which are Caesar's; and unto God the things that are God's."* They were disappointed in His answer. Jesus had slipped out of their noose one more time. Verse 22: *"When they had heard these words, they marvelled, and left him, and went their way."* Now Jesus knew that in a matter of days He was going to have to face Roman authority. He knew He was going to be facing Herod Antipas from Galilee. He did not face him in Galilee because Herod Antipas was in Jerusalem at the time of Jesus' trial. Pilate had had a dispute with Herod and they did not like each other. One was Jewish by religion and Edomite by race, and the other one was Roman and they hated one another. Over this tribute money issue and the allegiance to Rome they would come together at the time of the trial of Jesus and patch up their differences.

Luke 13:31 says: *"The same day there came certain of the Pharisees, saying unto him,* [The Pharisees came warning Jesus.] *Get thee out, and depart hence: for Herod will kill thee."* [He was in Galilee and Herod is over Galilee. The Pharisees are pretending to be His friend, telling Him to flee.] Verse 32, *"And he said unto them, Go ye, and tell that fox,* [Jesus knew that He would be facing that same fox in a matter of time.] *Behold, I cast out devils, and I do cures to day and to morrow, and the third day I shall be perfected.* [Listen to the profound answer of Jesus.] *Nevertheless I must walk to day, and to morrow,* [Jesus was leaving Galilee walking towards Jerusalem.] *and the day following: for it cannot be that a prophet perish out of Jerusalem."* He said "I am not worried about Roman authority. I am not worried about Herod in Galilee. **It is predestined that every prophet of God will die at the hands of the religious authorities in Jerusalem!"** This authority was responsible for the martyrdom of every prophet from Abel to Zachariah (Matthew 23:34-35).

THE SADDUCEES

Matthew 22:23: *"The same day came to him the Sadducees, which say that there is no resurrection, and asked him, Saying, Master. Moses said. If a man die, having no children, his brother shall marry his wife, and raise up seed unto his brother. Now there were with us seven brethren: and the first, when he had married a wife, deceased, and, having no issue, left his wife unto his brother: Likewise the second also, and the third, unto the seventh. And last of all the woman died also. Therefore in the resurrection whose wife shall she be of the seven? for they all had her."* This is a hypothetical question. The Sadducees who were asking this question did not even believe in the resurrection, but believed strictly in the written law. If there was nothing in the written Law of Moses about the resurrection or angels or any supernatural elements, they simply did not believe it. Therefore they cast it out of their theology and did not even consider it. They stuck to the strict interpretation of the law. They concocted this hypothetical question for Jesus to answer. It was a question of interpreting doctrine that they themselves did not even believe. They were aristocratic and nationalistic, and they held their position of authority in the religious life of the people. They felt threatened by Jesus. So they joined up with the other two groups to destroy our Lord.

Jesus' answer is found starting in verse 29: *"Jesus answered and said unto them, Ye do err, not knowing the scriptures, nor the power of God. For in the resurrection they neither marry, nor are given in marriage, but are as the angels of God in heaven. But as touching the resurrection of the dead, have ye not read that which was spoken unto you by God, saying, I am the God of Abraham, and the God of Isaac, and the God of Jacob? God is not the God of the dead, but of the living. And when the multitude heard this, they were astonished at his doctrine."* The Sadducees failed again to entrap the Savior.

THE PHARISEES

The Pharisees were a sect of self-righteous and zealous religious leaders who held to the strict interpretation of the Law, yet they added a lot of oral traditions to the body of the law. They then passed them down from generation to generation. This Rabbinical sect would get together and argue over the fine points of the law and come up with additional conclusions and regulations.

Matt. 22:34-37. *"But when the Pharisees had heard that he had put the Sadducees to silence, they were gathered together. Then one of them, which was a lawyer,* [a scribe, a thinker who can take something simple and make something complicated out of it] *asked him a question, tempting him, and saying, Master, which is the great commandment in the law. Jesus said unto him, Thou shalt love the Lord thy God with all thy heart, and with all thy soul, and with all thy mind."* They were disappointed in this answer because they were hoping to get Jesus caught in a quagmire of explanations trying to satisfy them and the spies in the crowd would go back to Herod. They wanted Him to choose allegiance between them and Herod. Jesus doesn't pick either one. Jesus said; *"Thou shalt love the Lord thy God with all thy heart, and with all thy soul, and with all thy mind. This is the first and great commandment. And the second is like unto it, Thou shalt love thy neighbour as thyself. On these two commandments hang all the law and the prophets."* He did not comment on the Pharisaical or the Roman law. The conniving Pharisees failed again.

JESUS' QUESTION

Now it is Jesus' turn. Matt. 22:41-45: *"While the Pharisees were gathered together, Jesus asked them, Saying, What think ye of Christ? Whose son is he? They say unto him, The Son of David. He saith unto them, How then doth David in spirit call him Lord, saying, The LORD said unto my Lord, Sit thou on my right hand, till I make thine enemies thy footstool. If David then call him Lord, how is he his son?.* He didn't say, 'what think ye of the Law or what think ye of the Roman authorities. He said, *'What think ye of Christ?'* That was the issue then and it is still the issue today. In essence Jesus was saying, Herodians, with your allegiance to the family, Sadducees, in your gross unbelief in the supernatural, Pharisees, with your hypocritical, egotistical approach and your self-righteousness, I want to bring all three of you together and say, 'What do you think of the Messiah?'

They answered saying, "Oh, the Messiah is the son of David." They are getting themselves in a trap. They knew the Scriptures. Then Jesus quoted something from David. Verse 43: *"He saith unto them, How then doth David in spirit call him Lord, saying, The LORD said unto my Lord, Sit thou on my right hand, till I make thine enemies thy footstool? If David then call him Lord, how is he his son?.* As we come to this juncture in Jesus' retaliatory question, He took them back to something that they knew absolutely nothing about: divine revelation. One of the great problems in American religion today is that we have forsaken revelation for human reasoning.

Jesus then said this, "Pharisees, you know nothing about divine revelation." In verse 44 Jesus quotes David from Psalm 110:1. *"The LORD said unto my Lord, Sit thou on my right hand, till I make thine enemies thy footstool. If David then called him Lord, how is he his son?"* As Jesus gave this short powerful answer, He then confirmed by self affirmation the following things. *1) He* was the Messiah; *2)* The Pharisees knew that Jesus was the Son of David; *3)* Christ existed before David; *4)* David had a divine revelation by the Holy Ghost; 5) David recognized Christ as his Lord; *6)* David was privy to a divine conversation. *"The Lord said unto my Lord." 7)* The Right Hand, the position of supreme authority was reserved for Jesus the Messiah and He alone; *8)* Christ will be victorious over all His enemies as He quoted in Psalm 110:1; *9)* Jesus is David's Lord in the spirit, but in the flesh He is David's son. Those three groups stood there with their heads swimming, because the record states, *"no man was able to answer Him a word and no man ask Him any questions after that."*

Psalm 110:1. *"The LORD said unto my Lord, Sit thou at my right hand, until I make thine enemies thy footstool."* That is not the end of the revelation that David received. That is only the part that Jesus quoted. David went on to say in verse two, *"The LORD shall send the rod of thy strength out of Zion: rule thou in the midst of thine enemies. Thy people shall be willing in the day of thy power, in the beauties of holiness from the womb of the morning: thou hast the dew of thy youth.* These three groups were asking a question from the

Levitical realm and Jesus gave them an answer from the Melchizedek realm. In His wisdom He avoided giving them a direct answer.

Psalm 110 declares: *1)* That there are enemies. *2)* Jesus is at the
right hand of authority. *3)* He is going to put His foot on them, as
though He is using them as a footstool. He has military, civil and
kingly authority. He will have a dual office and now He is going to
be priest. *"Thou art a priest for ever after the order of Melchizedek"*
(Heb. 5:6). Our Lord Jesus Christ holds that position as Melchizedek forever and He is the head and we are His body. That puts us
also into that realm of Melchizedek. We must keep our conduct
above reproach just as Jesus did. Don't give anyone a cause to
bring us into a place where they can say we have stooped to their
level. Once we do that, they have won. We must stand upon the
principle of divine revelation and no man knows this wonderful
truth outside of divine revelation. It is time we leave this realm of
Levitical quagmire behind us and ascend into a higher level with
our Lord Jesus Christ.

Melchizedek and the Blessing of Jacob
Chapter Eleven

Hebrews 11:21; *"By faith Jacob, when he was a dying, blessed both the sons of Joseph; and worshipped, leaning upon the top of his staff."* It was by faith that Jacob, at 147 years old, when dying blessed the sons of Joseph, Ephraim and Manasseh. In this blessing he was worshiping and leaning upon his staff while sitting on that Egyptian bed. This man by faith foresaw hundreds of years down through time as he crossed his arms and blessed those two boys.

We see a beautiful, wonderful prophetic story in the life of our forefather Jacob. He secured the family birthright and the blessing from his father Isaac in a deceptive way and due to his brother's anger over this deception, his mother advised him to leave home because his brother Esau had vowed to kill him. Genesis 27:41 says. *"And Esau hated Jacob because of the blessing wherewith his father blessed him: and Esau said in his heart, The days of mourning for my father are at hand; then will I slay my brother Jacob."* Esau's extreme hatred produced a deliberate design to slay his brother. Rebekah went to her favorite son and told him he had better leave home. She advised him to go to her father's house - to the place where he would be safe with his relatives. In Genesis 28:10 it says, *"And Jacob went out from Beersheba, and went toward Haran* [That is far northern Palestine, in present-day Syria.] *And he lighted upon a certain place, and tarried there all night, because the sun was set; and he took of the stones of that place, and put them for his pillows, and lay down in that place to sleep. And he dreamed, and behold a ladder set up on the earth, and the top of it reached to heaven: and behold the angels of God ascending and descending on it."*

There is a parallel between the life of Jacob and the life of Jesus. During this dream that Jacob saw, the angels were ascending and descending. In John 1:47-51 it says, *"Jesus saw Nathanael coming to him, and saith of him, Behold an Israelite indeed, in whom is no guile. Nathanael saith unto him, Whence knowest thou me? Jesus answered and said unto him, Before that Philip called thee, when thou wast under the fig tree, I saw thee. Nathanael answered and saith unto him, Rabbi, thou art the Son of God; thou art the King of Israel. Jesus answered and said unto him, Because I said unto thee, I saw thee under the fig tree, believest thou? Thou shalt see greater things than these. And he saith unto him, Verily, verily, I say unto you, Hereafter ye shall see heaven open, and the angels of God ascending and descending upon the Son of man."* Jacob saw the angels ascending and descending. Now Jesus is referring to Jacob's experience. He uses words that are typical or significant of divine revelation. Angels of God, messengers of the most High, were transporting messages from heaven to earth and visa versa. Jesus said to Nathanael, 'You are going to see the epitome of that in the life and ministry that I have here on this earth."

Genesis 28:13: *"And, behold, the LORD stood above it, and said, I am the LORD God of Abraham thy father, and the God of Isaac: the land whereon thou liest, to thee will I give it, and to thy seed;"* [Here is a voice coming out of that divine revelation, of the ascending and descending angels. It says,] *'And thy seed shall be as the dust of the earth, and thou shalt spread abroad to the west, and to the east, and to the north, and to the south: and in thee and in thy seed shall all the families of the earth be blessed.'* Verse 15: *"And, behold, I am with thee, and will keep thee in all places whither thou goest, and will bring thee again into this land; for I will not leave thee, until I have done that which I have spoken to thee of. And Jacob awaked out of his sleep, and he said, Surely the LORD is in this place; and I knew it not."*

Jacob had a divine revelation during the night. He did not recognize God was in that place when he placed his head on the rocky pillow the night before. He did not realize that this was the house of God. Jacob was running away from an uncomfortable situation. So was Saul of Tarsus when he was running away in his own sinfulness and rebellion. He did not know that particular spot on the road to Damascus was going to turn out to be the house of God. The house of God is wherever you meet the Lord. Jacob recognized this as he said 'the Lord is present in this place and I knew it not.'

Verse 17: *"And he was afraid, and said, How dreadful is this place! this is none other but the house of God, and this is the gate of heaven."* What is the gate of heaven. At the bottom of that ladder was the gate. ***Divine revelation in your life is the gateway to heaven.*** Most Christians go through life and never have a divine revelation of God. They never see a messenger of God or have a message from God.

A revelation is not something about you, it is something about the Lord. The Lord spoke to Jacob and identified Himself. Everything in our experience should be Christ-centered or theocentric instead of man-centered. Divine revelation reveals Him to us. Jacob called the name of that place Bethel, the house of God. This special place started out with just a stone. That stone became the house of God. In verse 11 the Scripture says he took of the stones of that place and made one of them his pillow. In 28:18, *" And Jacob rose up early in the morning, and took the stone that he had put for his pillows, and set it up for a pillar, and poured oil upon the top of it."* Where did Jacob get the idea to pour oil on the stone. This is the first mention in the Bible of pouring oil. Was this something that came to him in the night vision or was it something he had learned from his father Isaac, or Abraham his grandfather that consecrated this stone by pouring oil upon it.

We see this rite being practiced all the way throughout the Scriptures. Samuel took a horn of oil and poured it upon David's head. James said, *"Is any sick among you? let him call for the elders of the church; and let them pray over him, anointing him with oil in the name of the Lord"* (James 5:14). This practice is a 'family' tradition all the way back to Jacob. He turned this stone from a Pillow into a Pillar as he consecrated it. The word anoint means to 'pour oil upon.' Who is the stone. The Church of England says that Jacob's stone is the same one that reposed under the coronation chair in Westminster Abbey for many years and which is now in Scotland. Historically this is true, but who is the real stone? Was the real stone anointed. Jesus said, *'I am the stone that the builders rejected."* In Luke 4 He says, *'the spirit of the Lord is upon me because he hath anointed me'* (Luke 4:18). Oil was symbolically poured upon our Savior as the Holy Spirit descended on Him.

In Genesis 28:20 Jacob hears the words of God, based upon the divine revelation he had just heard from this heavenly voice. Jacob vowed a vow and obligated himself. He and his seed were included. When Jacob vowed the vow he included you and me as well. Verse 20: *"And Jacob vowed a vow, saying, If God will be with me, and will keep me in this way that I go, and will give me bread to eat, and raiment to put on,* [Jacob was scared as he ran from his brother.] *So that I come again to my father's house in peace; then shall the LORD be my God: And this stone, which I have set for a pillar, shall be God's house: and of all that thou shalt give me I will surely give the tenth unto thee."* Jacob locked us all into his vow. If you are a child of Jacob you are living under this vow.

Jacob went to Haran and arrived at his uncle's (his mother's brother) home. *"Then Jacob went on his journey, and came into the land of the people of the east. And he looked, and behold a well in the field, and, lo, there were three flocks of sheep lying by it; for out of that well they watered the flocks: and a great stone was upon the well's mouth. And thither were all the flocks gathered: and they rolled the stone from the well's mouth, and watered the sheep, and put the stone again upon the well's mouth in his place. And Jacob said unto them, My brethren, whence be ye? And they said, Of Haran are we. And he said unto them, Know ye Laban the son of Nahor?* [Abraham's brother] *And they said, We know him. And he said unto them, Is he well? And they said, He is well: and, behold. Rachel his daughter cometh with the sheep. And he said, Lo, it is yet high day,* [noon] *neither is it time that the cattle should be gathered together: water ye the sheep, and go and feed them. And they said, We cannot, until all the flocks be gathered together, and till they roll the stone from the well's mouth; then we water the sheep. And while he yet spake with them, Rachel came with her father's sheep: for she kept them. And it came to pass, when Jacob saw Rachel the daughter of Laban his mother's brother, and the sheep of Laban his mother's brother, that Jacob went near, and rolled the stone from the well's mouth, and watered the flock of Laban his mother's brother. And Jacob kissed Rachel, and lifted up his voice, and wept."*

He had never seen Rachel before, but he immediately loved her. Jacob told Rachel that he was of her same family, kissed her and wept for joy. He was overcome with the prompt answer to his expectation that he was going to be reunited with his family. Something within him was put there by divine providence so that he loved his own relatives. Jacob immediately pushed the stone away from the well's mouth and he watered the sheep for Rachel.

Genesis 32:1 *"And Jacob went on his way, and the angels of God met him."* This occurred after Jacob had spent many years working for his uncle Laban. Now he wanted to leave and be on his own and was going back home, but he had a problem. That problem was Esau. *"And Jacob went on his way, and the angels of God met him. And when Jacob saw them, he said, This is God's host:"* How did he recognize God's host. Were they the same angels who were ascending and descending on that ladder so long before?

Verse 3:1: *"And Jacob sent messengers before him to Esau his brother unto the land of Seir, the country of Edom."* He sent messengers to Esau with a peace offering, sending cattle and sheep to appease his angry brother. Jacob was desperate. When Jesus was desperate facing His 'Esau' so to speak, during His temptation in the wilderness, a dispatch of angels was sent to Him. It was the devil whom

Jesus met, but was the devil in the form of Pharisees, Sadducees, lawyers and scribes. Jesus was facing His Esau and His heavenly Father dispatched angels to minister to Him, just as He had to Jacob.

Genesis 32:22-28. *"And he rose up that night, and took his two wives, and his two womenservants, and his eleven sons, and passed over the ford Jabbok. And he took them, and sent them over the brook, and sent over that he had. And Jacob was left alone; and there wrestled a man with him until the breaking of the day."* [Jacob is having another encounter with God.] *And when he* [the angel] *saw that he prevailed not against him* [Jacob], *he touched the hollow of his thigh; and the hollow of Jacob's thigh was out of joint, as he wrestled with him. And he* [the angel] *said, Let me go, for the day breaketh. And he* [Jacob] *said, I will not let thee go, except thou bless me. And he said unto him, What is thy name? And he said, Jacob."* It says in verse 24 that there wrestled a **man** with Jacob. This man asked him 'What is your name?. Jacob answered and then this man gave a divine decree. *"And he said, Thy name shall be called no more Jacob, but Israel: for as a prince hast thou power with God and with men, and hast prevailed. And Jacob asked him, and said, Tell me, I pray thee, thy name. And he said, Wherefore is it that thou dost ask after my name. And he blessed him there."*

Before the Lord blessed him, He changed Jacob's name to Israel, "prince with God." Jacob has now been put into the capacity of Prince, holding civil authority. Verse 30 says, *"And Jacob called the name of the place Peniel: for I have seen God face to face, and my life is preserved."* Jacob identifies the man. **He said it was God!** He said he saw God face to face and his life was preserved. This was Jesus

Christ Himself. Imagine in this preincarnate state Jesus revealing Himself to our father Jacob. Jacob was actually wrestling with the Lord Jesus Christ Himself. Jesus had the authority to change Jacob's name. In the book of Acts, who changed Saul's name. . This also was not just an ordinary angel. When Jacob was at Luz he heard the voice of God. Now at Peniel he again hears the voice of God and even encounters Him physically and the Lord touches Jacob's thigh. He had to make Jacob lame to get him to release Him and let Him go. The sun rose upon them and Jacob halted upon his thigh. His meeting with Esau was preceded by a meeting with the Lord Jesus Christ Himself.

Jacob meets his brother Esau and in chapter 33:17-20 it says; *"And Jacob journeyed to Succoth, and built him an house, and made booths for his cattle: therefore the name of the place is called Succoth. And Jacob came to Shalem, a city of Shechem, which is in the land of Canaan, when he came from Padanaram; and pitched his tent before the city. And he bought a parcel of a field, where he had spread his tent, at the hand of the children of Hamor, Shechem's father, for an hundred pieces of money. And he erected there an altar, and called it Elelohe-Israel."* This man is functioning not only as a prince, but also as a priest as he built the altar. The building of the altars and the priest concept goes all the way back to Cain and Abel.

Before God could deal with Israel as a nation He had to deal with Jacob as a man. Three offices are operative in the Old Testament: **Prophet, Priest** and **King.** Jacob was anointed and appointed as prince and now he began to function as a priest. *Jacob the prince and Jacob the priest.* Genesis 35:6-7: *"So Jacob came to Luz, which is* *in the land of Canaan, that is, Bethel, he and all the people that were with him. And he built there an altar, and called the place Elbethel: because there God appeared unto him, when he fled from the face of his brother."* Jacob is fleeing again and comes back to Bethel, the house of God. He renames it Elbethel or the God of the house, for he was desperate again. Somebody was constantly after him. In verse 9, *"And God appeared unto Jacob again, when he came out of Padanaram, and blessed him."* Verse 10: *"And God said unto him, Thy name is Jacob: thy name shall not be called any more Jacob, but Israel shall be thy name: and he called his name Israel."* All of his sons had been born at this time except Benjamin, who was born after Jacob's name had been changed. This young lad was born under the authority of not just Jacob, but under the authority of Israel. Something special is to become of Benjamin - he is going to be a man of light and understanding.

Genesis 35:14: *"And Jacob set up a pillar in the place where he talked with him, [God] even a pillar of stone: and he poured a drink offering thereon, and he poured oil thereon."* This occurred at least two hundred years before Moses and the institution of offerings in Israel, yet Jacob knew about anointing with oil and the drink offering which was generally wine. Jacob is functioning as a priest long before Moses came along and before his son Levi was born and came into his calling with his family of priests. This came about by divine revelation.

Divine revelation comes to prophets. Jacob functioned as a prince, a priest and now as a prophet. There was authority in Jacob. In Genesis 48 Jacob is an old man and his eyes are dim, but he gives

Joseph a charge in Gen. 47:29-31: "*And the time drew nigh that Israel must die: and he called his son Joseph, and said unto him, If now I have found grace in thy sight, put, I pray thee, thy hand under my thigh,* [This was an indication of a most solemn vow between two people.] *and deal kindly and truly with me; bury me not, I pray thee, in Egypt: But I will lie with my fathers, and thou shalt carry me out of Egypt, and bury me in their burying place. And he said, I will do as thou hast said. And he said, Swear unto me. And he sware unto him. And Israel bowed himself upon the bed's head.*"

Word came to Joseph that his father was sick and on his death-bed. Genesis 48:1: "*And it came to pass after these things, that one told Joseph, Behold, thy father is sick: and he took with him his two sons, Manasseh and Ephraim. And one told Jacob, and said, Behold, thy son Joseph cometh unto thee: and Israel strengthened himself, and sat upon the bed. And Jacob said unto Joseph, God Almighty appeared unto me at Luz in the land of Canaan, and blessed me,* [God Almighty blessed Jacob—it was not just an angel.] *And said unto me, Behold, I will make thee fruitful, and multiply thee, and I will make of thee a multitude of people; and will give this land to thy seed after thee for an everlasting possession.*"

Jacob crossed his arms and blessed these two sons of Joseph. He put his right hand upon the younger boy's head and his left hand upon the older boy's head. What was significant about this blessing. What about this family's birthright? Joseph thought that his father would bless them in the customary manner and give the greater blessing to the older son. But Jacob was guiding his hands purposefully and some of the words he said are recorded in verse 15: "*And he blessed*

Joseph, and said, God, before whom my fathers Abraham and Isaac did walk, the God which fed me all my life long unto this day."

The reference to Abraham and Isaac was a reference to the covenants God had given to Abraham. Jacob continued, *"the God that fed me all my life long."* He recognized God as the One who shepherded him. This word **"fed"** means to shepherd. The shepherd does more than just give food to the sheep; he leads them in paths of safety and righteousness. He leads them away from the poison weeds and leads them into rich pasture. He led Jacob all the days of his life and now Jacob is identifying God as a God of divine provision. First, He is recognized as the God of Covenants and now as a God of divine provision. Then in verse 16 he says 'angel'. In the King James the word angel is capitalized. *"The Angel which redeemed me from all evil, bless the lads; and let my name be named on them, and the name of my fathers Abraham and Isaac; and let them grow into a multitude in the midst of the earth."*

What evil is Jacob talking about now? The evil of Esau, of Laban and of the Shechemites. This angel mentioned in verse 16 is the same God of Abraham and Isaac of verse 15. He says the "angel" that redeemed me. The word "redemption" means to repossess something that already belonged to you. This angel was blood kin to Jacob, because this is kinsman-redemption. This 'angel' that Jacob was wrestling with was none other than his kinsman-Redeemer, the Lord Jesus Christ. We see Jacob identifying this Person as God. He is going to invoke His name on these two sons. Jacob identifies God as the God of Abraham and Isaac, with covenant-making and covenant-keeping power. He identifies this God as the God of provision and now as their Redeemer. Then he pronounces an unconditional blessing on these boys which could not be revoked or overridden by the Mosaic covenant. The blessing of Jacob upon these boys even overrides the conditions of their disobedience under the Law of Moses. He utters this by divine decree. What gave Jacob this authority. When he wrestled with an "angel" (Jesus Christ), met God face to face, (Gen. 2:24) God spoke to Jacob and said his name was no longer *'deceiver'* and supplanter. God was putting something into his genetic makeup. He established not only something in his life but also in those of his offspring.

THE ADOPTION OF EPHRAIM AND MANASSEH

The adoption of Ephraim and Manasseh was by divine oath. This reminds us of another occasion in Genesis 14, when a Man blessed Abram by divine oath and again in Hebrews 7 where those who received this office received it by divine oath. Could it be that Jacob had this Melchizedek calling on him. Perhaps this blessing had been passed down to him and he was the Melchizedek of his day. He was functioning in this role long before Moses was born. He was building altars and receiving divine revelations and his name had been changed to 'a prince' with God. . The three-fold offices of the Old Testament had now been placed in this man and he was going to pass this same blessing on to his children.

This blessing that Jacob gave to his two grandchildren derived from the role and responsibility of the Melchizedek office and not the Levitical office. In Genesis 48:5 Jacob is talking to Joseph: *"And now thy two sons, Ephraim and Manasseh, which were born unto thee in the land of Egypt before I came unto thee into Egypt, are mine; as Reuben and Simeon, they shall be mine."* He was saying, 'Joseph, these two sons of yours are now mine.' Just as much as Reuben and Simeon, they shall be mine. Gen. 48:16 goes on: *"... and let my name be named on them, and the name of my fathers Abraham and Isaac; and let them grow into a multitude in the midst of the earth."* **Let my name be named on them. This is adoption.** Whom did Jacob adopt. His own blood kin. This is the Biblical principle of adoption.

Before Jacob could bless those boys he had to adopt them. Adoption as recounted in this chapter is a four-step process. *1. The imposition of hands* or the laying on of hands. Verse 14: *"And Israel stretched out his right hand, and laid it upon Ephraim's head, who was the younger, and his left hand upon Manasseh's head, guiding his hands wittingly; for Manasseh was the firstborn."* *2) The invocation of a higher authority.* To invoke the name of supreme authority, he said in verse 15. *"... God, before whom my fathers Abraham and Isaac did walk, the God which fed me all my life long unto this day, and the angel which redeemed me."* He identified this authority as the God of **covenant**, the God of **provision** and the God of **redemption**. *3) The declaration of adoption.* Jacob said, 'These two sons of Joseph are mine, let my name be named upon them." *4) Then came the last step, the blessing. "... and let them grow into a multitude in the midst of the earth."* He didn't just bless those boys at random. He had to go through a divine process.

In Galatians 4, the Apostle Paul is writing to the Galatians, who were Israelites of the dispersion. Galatians 4:1: *"Now I say, That the heir, as long as he is a child, differeth nothing from a servant, though he be lord of all; But is under tutors and governors until the time appointed of the father. Even so we, when we were children, were in bondage under the elements of the world:"* He is talking to a congregation of Israelites known as the Galatians who were part of the dispersion of the ten tribes. Verse 4, *"But when the fulness of the time was come, God sent forth his Son, made of a woman, made under the law, To redeem them that were under the law, that we might receive the adoption of sons."*

Whom did Jesus redeem. He redeemed those who were already under the law. Verse 6: *"And because ye are sons, God hath sent forth the Spirit of his Son into your hearts, crying, Abba, Father."* Take this New Testament verse and apply it to Jacob and that incident in Genesis 48. Jacob could have just as easily said this: 'Ephraim and Manasseh, I am going to adopt you just as much as the other boys are mine and because you are already sons I am going to put this blessing upon you." Paul puts it in New Testament language saying, *"And because ye are sons, God hath sent forth the Spirit of his Son into your hearts, crying, Abba, Father."* Ephraim and Manasseh can turn to Jacob now and instead of saying grandfather they can say, 'You are our father.' That is the **Biblical concept of adoption.** Jacob put these two boys into the status of sons. Jesus Christ came and brought into a higher realm and status of sonship those who were once scattered and aliens of the house of Israel. He brought them up to the level of full sonship.

Adam Clarke's commentary says. "The angel which redeemed me from all evil. The messenger or redeemer or kinsman. (Goel): This term in the law of Moses is applied to that person whose right it is from his being nearest of kin to redeem or purchase back a forfeited inheritance." But of whom does Jacob speak. We have often seen an angel of God appearing to the patriarchs. We have full proof that this was no created angel but the messenger of the divine counsel, the Lord Jesus Christ. Who then was the angel who redeemed Jacob and whom he invoked in blessing Ephraim and Manasseh. Is it not Jesus. He alone can be called 'Goel,' the kinsman-redeemer, for He alone took the part of our flesh and blood so that the right of redemption might be His. The forfeited possession of the favor and image of God was brought back, restored to all who believe in His name. To invoke any other angel or messenger in such a proceeding would have been the grossest impiety. Angels bless not, for this prerogative belongs to God alone. With great confidence a true father may use these words in behalf of his children, "Jesus the Christ, who hath redeemed me, bless the lads. Redeem them also and save them unto eternal life."

Jacob was blessed as a prophet, a priest and as a king long before these offices were manifested in his offspring. Jacob was filling a Melchizedek office.

Melchizedek's Greatest Offer
Chapter Twelve

In John, chapters 13 through 17, we can read Jesus' Passover sermon. This is the part that is seldom mentioned or connected with Passover, the Passover meal or the whole Passion week. These chapters have been distorted and interpreted to be a 'selfish' Gospel. In John 14 Jesus said He had mansions in His Father's house, but some interpretations have held that Jesus was referring to the 'rapture', and that is the first mention of rapture in the Bible. Is this a valid interpretation of the passage, and if so, what is it based on. This is not a veiled prediction of an alleged rapture. This passage of Scripture is Melchizedek's greatest offer to His disciples. Why do I say Melchizedek. Because Aaron could not make these offers. Levi could not suffice for anything except to satisfy the demands of the holiness of God according to the Old Covenant. When it came to making a new covenant, Levi was ordained to fail. Only Melchizedek could make the glorious offers that we find in these chapters.

In some circles, these chapters have been used to promote a 'mud hut' religion centered on a false piety. *"Lord just build me a cabin in the corner of Glory Land."* That is false piety and it has also been used as the image of an unfounded state of hopeful bliss. *"Lord build me a mansion over the hilltop."* That is egotism. What did Jesus mean? John 13 holds the greatest offer that Jesus ever made to His disciples. This wonderful message is part of their Passover observance. Jesus gave this great discourse and made this overwhelming offer as part of this important Feast. From the time their Passover meal was finished to the time they reached the Garden of Gethsemane, they were walking and talking together. John says they crossed over a brook called Kidron, which is the same brook that King David crossed over a thousand years earlier when he was running from his pursuers. Jesus crossed this same brook, while His pursuer was actually conspiring against Him. At that point Jesus was actually speaking with his disciples and telling them some wonderful things to recall later after He had returned to Heaven.

Four questions in this chapter are important for us to consider: Peter's question, Thomas' statement, Philip's query, and Judas' problem. This man is not the traitor Judas Iscariot, but Judas the brother of James.

John 13:31-34: *"Therefore, when he* [Judas Iscariot] *was gone out, Jesus said, Now is the Son of man glorified, and God is glorified in him. If God be glorified in him, God shall also glorify him in himself, and shall straightway glorify him. Little children, yet a little while I am with you. Ye shall seek me: and as I said unto the Jews, Whither I go, ye cannot come; so now I say to you. A new commandment I give unto you, That ye love one another; as I have loved you, that ye also love one another."* Judas Iscariot has been made known as the traitor. He was revealed as the one who was going to betray his Lord to the authorities. The apprehension was building up among the remaining disciples. They were thinking, 'Oh no, this is the time we have been dreading. This is the time we thought would never come, but it is right here. Jesus is going to be betrayed into the hand of sinners and what are we going to do?'. They feared the Roman Empire, which was a valid fear, but they had an even greater fear of the Jews, as John's account brings out so clearly. Then Jesus said to them, 'This is the commandment I am giving you. I am going to give you a new commandment, a new charge, a new admonition: you had better stick together.' He said, *"That you love one another"* to the extent that He had expressed His love toward them.

John 13:1: *"... having loved his own which were in the world, he loved them unto the end."* To what extent did He love them. He loved them to the end. If that is the extent to which He loved His disciples, He was telling them that is the extent He wanted them to love one another as well. 'I want you to love one another to the very end and this is going to be the distinguishing mark that will show men that you are My disciples.' John 13:35 says: *"By this shall all men know that ye are my disciples, if ye have love one to another."*

Now the Lord had loved Peter in spite of Peter's remarks and rebuke to Him. He had loved all His disciples in their egotism, as one desired to sit on His left and the other on His right. He has to love us through all our own faults as well. All of our boasting, pride and religious ego: He has to love us through all that and He does. This incident is where He really shows His love to the disciples. In John 15:13, He tells them, *"Greater love hath no man than this, that a man lay down his life for his friends."* 'So therefore I am giving you this charge that you love one another with the kind of love that I have expressed to you.' Now this was perplexing to the disciples. They still did not know what the plan of God was and what Jesus had in mind.

THE FIRST QUESTION: PETER

The words of Jesus in John 13:33 prompted a serious question from the Apostle Peter. *"Little children, yet a little while I am with you. Ye shall seek me: and as I said unto the Jews, Whither I go, ye cannot come; so now I say to you."* In verse 36, Peter picks up on this: *"Simon Peter said unto him, Lord, whither goest thou? Jesus answered him, Whither I go, thou canst not follow me now; but thou shalt follow me afterwards."* At one time I was taught that Jesus was referring to the ascension; that He was going away and later will come back in what is termed the 'rapture' and take Peter with Him. But that does not adequately interpret the text. He is saying, 'Peter, you are not man enough to follow Me now. You cannot follow Me in suffering and in death. You are now unable to do it, but someday you will be able to follow Me in suffering and in death.' He was not talking about the rapture of the church or the ascension. He was talking about going to the cross. In verse 31, He said 'I am going to be glorified.' His death is the way by which the Son of Man would be glorified. He had said all men would be drawn unto Him if He was lifted up. He was talking about His crucifixion.

In verse 37: *"Peter said unto him, Lord, why cannot I follow thee now? I will lay down my life for thy sake."* Peter wasn't speaking in terms of going to another planet; he was talking in terms of Jesus' crucifixion and death. Peter said, 'I can and I will, I will even lay down my life for you.' *"Jesus answered him, Wilt thou lay down thy life for my sake?* [Yes, you will but not now.] *verily, verily, I say unto thee, The cock shall not crow, till thou hast denied me thrice."*

This was a very personal conversation, face to face, while walking to the Garden. The Lord exposed the heart of Peter in front of the other ten disciples. 'Peter, do you think you can follow Me now. You don't realize what you're saying. You really don't know the plan, but you will know the plan when you follow Me in suffering and in death.'

The key to Peter's answer goes back to John 13:1, emphasizing Jesus' love for them. He knew their weaknesses and their feelings of apprehension, because He knew the Scripture where the prophet said, 'Smite the shepherd and the sheep shall scatter.' He knew the scattering had to take place and He knew Peter was one who would scatter. Then He told them, 'You love one another.' At this particular point Jesus never mentioned the world. When Jesus was talking to these eleven men He said, 'You love one another.' He did not say, 'You love the world and everybody in the world.' That is misplaced love. First each one of us has to learn this intimate, organic connection with Jesus Christ and the other believers. Therein is the expression of God's greatest love.

They were still walking from the Upper Room to the Garden of Gethsemane. No doubt this took approximately an hour or maybe two. He undoubtedly said a lot of things that were not recorded, but we know that Jesus was making His greatest offer to His disciples and this offer starts with the quality of Godly love.

Now the disciples were all afraid for the fear of the unknown was overtaking their minds. The fury against Jesus was building in

Jerusalem. Judas was busy doing his work, conspiring with the High Priests and the other evil men of that day. The Roman government was at the place where they were between a rock and a hard place, since they had to decide their official course of action concerning this man Jesus. The disciples knew this and were wondering if the government was looking for them as well. They knew when the Temple hierarchy looked at Jesus they were looking at them also. At this point the disciples in the garden decided to scatter, for their hearts were troubled. Jesus began to comfort them. He said, "*Let not your heart be troubled: ye believe in God, believe also in me.*" 'You believe in God, the Old Testament record, the Psalms and the Law, believe also in Me, because in My father's 'kingdom' are many dwelling places.' The King James Version says, "*In my Father's house are many mansions:*" Melchizedek is making a great offer to the disciples of the first century and across the years to us. He is saying, 'Let not your heart be disturbed. In fact it is my Father's good pleasure to give you the kingdom. There are dwelling places in that kingdom and you have a place.'

Why did He make this statement? 'I would not have led you to believe all of this if it were not true. What I am saying to you is true. Don't think that I have deceived you and told you that you have a place in My Father's kingdom and then it will not come to pass. If it were not true I would have told you a long time ago.' He said, 'I go to prepare a place for you.' Jesus is not up there with hammer, nails and boards building us a mansion. Do you know how He is preparing a place for us. He went to the cross. He said this is My blood of the New Covenant. He was ratifying a NEW Covenant with the House of Judah and the House of Israel.

THE SECOND QUESTION: THOMAS

John 14:3 continues; *"And if I go and prepare a place for you, I will come again, and receive you unto myself; that where I am, there ye may be also."* He was promising them, 'I will put you in the same glorified state that I will be in.' *"And whither I go ye know, and the way ye know. Thomas saith unto him, Lord, we know not whither thou goest; and how can we know the way?.* Thomas asked a two-part question. How do we know where You are going and how can we know the way. Jesus answered the question with, "I am the Way." Jesus was saying 'I am the Mediation. I am the Truth, I am the Personification of Divine Truth. Jesus said, I am the Source of your life. I am the epitome of all divine revelation, the source and maintenance of your life.' John 14:6 and 7 continues: *"Jesus saith unto him, I am the way, the truth, and the life: no man cometh unto the Father, but by me. If ye had known me, ye should have known my Father also: and from henceforth ye know him, and have seen him."*

THE THIRD QUESTION: PHILIP

"Philip saith unto him, Lord, shew us the Father, and it sufficeth us." Philip said, 'Show us the Father.' 'We have known You, Lord, and You should have shown us the Father. Now show us the Father and it will satisfy us.' *"Jesus saith unto him, Have I been so long time with you, and yet hast thou not known me, Philip? he that hath seen me hath seen the Father;"*

These men were dull of hearing, but so are we. We would have probably asked Jesus the same questions. The disciples had been

with Him for three and a half years and He told them they should
have seen the Father. Jesus had been expressing the Father all
that time. Yet they asked Him to show them the Father. He had
said, 'I and my Father are one.' Then Jesus asked this question:
"Believest thou not that I am in the Father, and the Father in me?
[Don't you believe I am in the Father?] *The words that I speak
unto you I speak not of myself: but the Father that dwelleth in me,
he doeth the works. Believe me that I am in the Father, and the
Father in me: or else believe me for the very works' sake."* Jesus was
making this offer and giving these comforting words during the
time of their darkest hour of despair. Jesus was giving promises
of the greatest hope. Beginning in John 14, He showed them the
organic connection between Himself and His Father.

First, Jesus described the organic connection between the Son and
the Father. Then He turned to these eleven men and said, *"Verily,
verily, I say unto you, He that believeth on me, the works that I do
shall he do also; and greater works than these shall he do; because
I go unto my Father. And whatsoever ye shall ask in my name, that
will I do.* In whose name did the Son come. He said, 'I came in
My Father's Name.' 'There is My Father's Name and here is My
Name and I have come in that same Name and there is authority
in that Name.' *"And whatsoever ye shall ask in my name, that will
I do, that the Father may be glorified in the Son. If ye shall ask any
thing in my name, I will do it."* He took the disciples and us into
the equation when He said, 'It is the Father and the Son and now
if you believe in Me, you are part of this equation with the Father
and the Son. Whatsoever ye shall ask, you need to ask it in the
authority of My Name. If you ask anything in My Name I will do it.'

Then Jesus described the principle of love again. Love is not true love unless obedience is contained in that love. Verse 15 commands: *"If ye love me, keep my commandments."* He gave them His new commandment when He said, *"If ye love me, keep my commandments. And I will pray the Father, and he shall give you another Comforter, that he may abide with you for ever;.* This word 'comforter' in the King James translation comes from the Greek word **parakletos.** 'Para' means along side of and 'kletos' means to call for help. He said, ' I am going away, but I am going to send you another comforter that He may abide with you for ever, and take up His abode with you.' Abode means residence, mansion and dwelling places. 'In My Father's house are many places of abode.' This place is not ten trillion miles away. Jesus was giving them the greatest gift of all, the offer of the Holy Spirit. He said, 'My Father and I will take up an abode with you. I am going to live in you permanently.'

John 14:17: *"Even the Spirit of truth; whom the world cannot receive, because it seeth him not, neither knoweth him: but ye know him; for he dwelleth with you, and shall be in you."* Truth comes by divine revelation. Jesus said, I am the truth and the Spirit that comes is the Spirit of truth. The Holy Spirit will speak of Jesus. He said, *"If ye shall ask any thing in my name, I will do it. If ye love me, keep my commandments."* He put the word 'if ' in there, and that was for us. Maybe we don't love to the extent that He loved His own. The love that Jesus was talking about was divine love, able to love His disciples unto the end and transform them into His likeness.

John 14:17 continues: *"Even the Spirit of truth; whom the world cannot receive, because it seeth him not, neither knoweth him: but ye know him; for he dwelleth with you, and shall be in you.*" Have I believed on the name of Jesus Christ. Have I loved to this same extent? Has the Holy Spirit been placed in me. What is truth. How does truth come. The Holy Spirit comes in His fullness, but He does not tell us everything in the beginning. Truth is progressively revealed to us as we seek it over our lifetimes. We cannot understand it all at once. This word *'comforter'* means teacher, advocate, consoler, guide, director and protector. Levi and his descendants could not make these offers.

Then Jesus promises in John 14:18: *"I will not leave you comfortless: I will come to you."* Now Jesus had previously said, 'I am going to come back to you, Peter.' How did He come back. He came back through His Holy Spirit that descended on the Day of Pentecost. The benefits of loving Jesus and obeying His commandments are many; the Spirit of truth or revelation of truth being in us and not being left without a comforter. Jesus made the statement, 'The Holy Spirit is come into you' and then He turns around and says I will come to you. The Holy Spirit is Jesus Christ in spirit form. Jesus Christ comes to each of us in the Spirit. The Holy Spirit is sometimes described as the promise of the Father or the Spirit of truth, the Spirit of understanding. It is by Spirit that we are joined unto Him and to His Father.

THE FOURTH QUESTION: JUDAS THADDEUS

He continued: (John 14:20): *"At that day ye shall know that I am in my Father, and ye in me, and I in you."* A wonderful trinity is described here. We are part of the divine trinity of God. Jesus is saying, 'My Father, Me and you.' And He said, 'You are going to be in Me and I am going to be in you. Verse 21, "*He that hath my commandments, and keepeth them, he it is that loveth me: and he that loveth me shall be loved of my Father, and I will love him, and will manifest myself to him.*" Then Judas, who is sometimes known as Thaddeus, had a question in verse 22. "*Judas saith unto him, not Iscariot, Lord, how is it that thou wilt manifest thyself unto us, and not unto the world.* When the Lord reveals a truth He is manifesting Himself. Let's not separate truth from the person of Jesus Christ. A revealed truth should humble us, for it is a manifestation of Jesus Christ. We should not be exalted by truth given to us. If we really heard His voice it would say the same thing He said to Jacob, "Thou worm." Jesus said, 'I am the epitome of divine revelation of knowledge and truth.' Our focus and our priority must be a person, and that Person is the Lord Jesus, not us.

"*Jesus answered and said unto him, If a man love me, he will keep my words: and my Father will love him, and we will come unto him, and make our abode with him.*" Jesus told Judas (Thaddeus) 'If a man loves Me he will keep My words.' That is the key to this whole Christian walk. "*He that loveth me not keepeth not my sayings: and the word which ye hear is not mine, but the Father's which sent me.*" The concept that is not taught here is that a person can say he loves Jesus and go out and live as he wants to live. Jesus says, 'He that loves Me not, keeps not My sayings or commandments.' "*These things have I spoken unto you, being yet present with you. But the Comforter, which is the Holy Ghost, whom the Father will send in my name, he shall teach you all things, and bring all things to your remembrance, whatsoever I have said unto you.*"

Then He says, 'My gift to you is; *"Peace I leave with you, my peace I give unto you: not as the world giveth, give I unto you. Let not your heart be troubled, neither let it be afraid."* In essence Jesus said; "Even though I am going to be falsely accused, persecuted and rejected. I am giving you My peace." **Peace for a child of God does not mean absence of trouble. It is rather the presence of Jesus Christ for all times and in every situation.** This peace is not outward, it is inward. He defines this peace as, My peace. Why do I say this is Melchizedek's greatest offer. One reason is found in Hebrews 7:2, where it reports: *"To whom* [Melchizedek] *also Abraham gave a tenth part of all; first being by interpretation King of righteousness, and after that also King of Salem, which is, King of peace;"* **Melchizedek was the King of Peace.** Jesus is saying, "I am giving you peace. Even though I face suffering and death, I have peace and I want to give that peace to you. You will need this peace. Let not your heart be troubled."

Jesus and His disciples were still enroute to the Garden and He ended their walk by saying: *"Ye have heard how I said unto you, I go away, and come again unto you. If ye loved me, ye would rejoice, because I said, I go unto the Father: for my Father is greater than I. And now I have told you before it come to pass, that, when it is come to pass, ye might believe. Hereafter I will not talk much with you: for the prince of this world cometh, and hath nothing in me.* [My accusers really have nothing against Me.] *But that the world may know that I love the Father; and as the Father gave me commandment, even so I do. Arise, let us go hence."* He knew what He was facing, but was concerned with His disciples and was reassuring them.

This is Melchizedek's greatest offer to us today. He invites us to be organically and spiritually connected to Him. He said, ask anything in My Name. Asking in His Name means more than just saying, "in Jesus Name" at the end of prayers. It is more than just calling His Name when we are in a tight spot. He gave us some commandments: Love, obedience, unity with Him and the Father so that we come under the authority of that Name. What He offered to the disciples there in the Garden He has offered to each one of us. He has offered us His best. We are in His kingdom, in His Father's house. We are *'the places'* of abode. Look upon yourself as a mansion in the Father's house. Where does the Father abide. Jesus was talking personally and He said to His disciples, 'You eleven men are the mansions or abiding places in My Father's house.'

Melchizedek - The Vineyard's True Vine
Chapter Thirteen

In the 15th chapter of John's Gospel we read Jesus' Passover discourse to His disciples. John 15:1 *"I am the true vine, and my Father is the husbandman."* Jesus was celebrating the last Passover He would observe with His disciples. The message that has been given by our Lord has been misunderstood, neglected and has often times been changed in its meaning by well-intentioned men. As our Lord began chapter 15, He said, *"I am the true vine, and My Father is the husbandman."* This is often strictly spiritualized. What is the root or background of our Lord's statement? Its emphasis spotlights the fact that this is both *a kingdom parable and a spiritual parable*. We must realize that our Lord was talking about the Kingdom throughout the major part of His teaching ministry.

This fifteenth chapter was recorded by John who was personally there, as an eyewitness. He was the man who was the closest in relationship with our Lord. He was the man who put his head on our Savior's breast. He was the man who could turn to our Savior with the request of Peter and the other disciples who wanted to know, 'Who is the traitor among us?' They knew he was the one who would most likely get the answer. John was at the Sea of Galilee in Matthew 3 and who, with his brother James, heard Jesus' call: *'Come and follow me and I will make you fishers of men.'* He stood on the Mount of Transfiguration with Jesus. Undoubtedly he was with the Lord constantly for three and a half years. He was one of the three who went into the room of the girl who died and watched as Jesus took her by the hand and said, *'Maiden arise.'*

John had a perspective of our Lord that the other disciples did not have. He had a personal and visible perspective with spiritual insight.

THE LORD'S VINEYARD

As we consider this parable of the True Vine, we realize that there are five trees or plants listed in parable form as representing God's people. First, there is the *fig* tree of corrupted Judah. There is the *olive* tree of engrafted Israel, as recorded by Paul in Romans. Then there is *wheat*. Jesus said the wheat are the children of the kingdom. Then there is a grape *vineyard*. Then within that vineyard is a *fruitful bough.*

Isaiah 5:1-7 says: *"Now will I sing to my wellbeloved a song of my beloved touching his vineyard. My wellbeloved hath a vineyard in a very fruitful hill. And he fenced it, and gathered out the stones thereof, and planted it with the choicest vine, and built a tower in the midst of it, and also made a winepress therein: and he looked that it should bring forth grapes, and it brought forth wild [sour] grapes. And now, O inhabitants of Jerusalem, and men of Judah, judge, I pray you, betwixt me and my vineyard. What could have been done more to my vineyard, that I have not done in it? wherefore, when I looked that it should bring forth grapes, brought it forth wild grapes?"* This is the expression of divine disappointment. He did everything He could do to this vineyard and yet it brought forth wild grapes. He even planted it with the choicest vines, to no avail.

Isaiah continues: *"And now go to; I will tell you what I will do to my vineyard: I will take away the hedge thereof, and it shall be eaten up;*

and break down the wall thereof, and it shall be trodden down: And
I will lay it waste: it shall not be pruned, nor digged; but there shall
come up briers and thorns: I will also command the clouds that they
rain no rain upon it." Then he tells us who the vineyard is. *"For the*
vineyard of the LORD of hosts is the house of Israel, and the men of
Judah his pleasant plant: and he looked for judgment [justice], *but*
behold oppression; for righteousness, but behold a cry [of distress]."
Therefore, when we read the Gospel story and it tells us that Jesus
gave a parable about a vineyard, we automatically know who that
vineyard is. It is the House of Israel and the House of Judah.

In Jeremiah 2:21 we read. *"Yet I had planted thee a noble vine, wholly*
a right seed: how then art thou turned into the degenerate plant of
a strange vine unto me?" They were planted as a noble vine and a
righteous seed, but they turned into a degenerate plant, sinful and
lawbreaking. That is the Scripture's description of the House of
Israel and the House of Judah. In Jeremiah 12:10 we read: *"Many*
pastors have *destroyed my vineyard, they have trodden my portion*
under foot, they have made my pleasant portion a desolate wilder-
ness." The Scriptures are talking about the vineyard of the House
of the Lord.

JOSEPH – THE FRUITFUL BOUGH

When the aged patriarch Jacob began to bless his sons he blessed
Joseph with the birthright. Joseph was the oldest son of his beloved
wife, Rachel, although he was not Jacob's firstborn son. A whole
vineyard, the whole house of Israel and the whole house of Judah,
lie before us. Imagine a circle inside a circle and we realize he is

emphasizing a particular part of the vineyard. The bough of this particular vine is very fruitful and is going to multiply in people. It is a *fruitful bough*. For emphasis, he uses that as a redundant phrase. This is what Jacob said to Joseph: *"Joseph is a fruitful bough, even a fruitful bough by a well* [running water or nourishment]; *whose branches run over the wall:"* The picture is that there is a wall or an enclosed area where this vine is planted. It is going to grow so plentifully that it is going to spill over the wall or beyond its original bounds.

Every Bible scholar knows this is talking about the posterity of Joseph. His people are going to multiply with a special blessing on them. As we trace the descendants of Joseph in the natural as the true **House of Israel**, we recognize this branch that has grown beyond its borders. These people have greatly increased in history. This passage is also describing material and spiritual blessings to be given to Joseph. Verse 23 continues: *"The archers have sorely grieved him, and shot at him, and hated him. But his bow abode in strength, and the arms of his hands were made strong by the hands of the mighty God of Jacob; (from thence is the shepherd, the stone of Israel:).* The Shepherd is identified with this particular branch of this big vineyard of the Lord of Hosts. Jesus Christ is truly the stone of Israel, the chief cornerstone upon which the national and spiritual house is built.

Our focus is the Lord Jesus Christ. We have seen how the blessing of this patriarch Joseph descended from the greater patriarch, Jacob, resulting in his seed producing a **savior**, a **shepherd**, and a **cornerstone**. Verse 25 continues. *"Even by the God of thy father, who shall* *help thee; and by the Almighty, who shall bless thee with blessings of heaven above, blessings of the deep that lieth under, blessings of the breasts, and of the womb:.* A special material blessing was imparted to this particular vine.

In Psalm 80 we read these beautiful words: *"Give ear, O Shepherd of Israel, thou that leadest Joseph like a flock;"* The writer identifies Joseph as the one of whom he is speaking and is identifying the Shepherd of Israel leading Joseph. Therefore we see the Shepherd of Israel is going to lead Joseph like a flock. Then verse 8: *"Thou hast brought a vine out of Egypt: thou hast cast out the heathen, and planted it.* [Planted what? This noble vine.] *Thou preparedst room before it, and didst cause it to take deep root, and it filled the land. The hills were covered with the shadow of it, and the boughs thereof were like the goodly cedars. She sent out her boughs unto the sea, and her branches unto the river."*

In other words, these people went all the way across Assyria, between the Caspian and Black Seas, across the Caucasus Mountains, continued north and west and covered the face of the earth. They went all the way to the North Sea. They crossed that stretch of water to Great Britain and migrated until they reached the shores of Massachusetts. There they signed a compact that states they were coming here for the Kingdom of God and the Gospel of Jesus Christ. The Shepherd of Israel was among them. The whole vine did not come, but the special bough of Joseph came. The Shepherd and the Stone of Israel led them like a flock. God brought a vine out of Egypt. We read: *"Why hast thou then broken down her hedges, so that all they which pass by the way do pluck her. The boar out of the wood doth waste it, and the wild beast of the field doth devour it* [That is the history of Europe]. *Return, we beseech thee, O God of hosts: look down from heaven, and behold, and visit this vine; And the vineyard which thy right hand hath planted,* [Who planted it. God Almighty.] *and the branch that thou madest strong for thyself. It is burned with fire, it is cut down: they perish at the rebuke of thy countenance.*" Our prayer is: Lord, visit this vine once again.

JESUS - THE CHOICE VINE

We here observe this special vine, the House of Joseph and the identification of the Savior and the Stone. First, we had the **whole vineyard**, then we had a **special bough**, the House of Joseph, but now we have something further. In Genesis 49:10, as Jacob gave the blessing unto Judah, he said: *"The sceptre shall not depart from Judah, nor a lawgiver from between his feet,* [from his loins, his seed or posterity] until *Shiloh come; and unto him shall the gathering of the people be."* Those are the rest of the tribes of Israel that will gather unto Him. Verse 11: *"Binding his foal unto the vine, and his ass's colt unto the choice vine; he washed his garments in wine, and his clothes in the blood of grapes:"* We first see a **vineyard**, then a **fruitful bough** of the House of Joseph and then a **choice vine** among them.

That Choice Vine, who is Jesus Christ, is speaking in John 15. He said, *"I am the choice vine."* Do you see the connection with the birthright blessing of Joseph and the sceptre blessing of Judah. In both of them Jacob mentioned something about a vine: A **fruitful bough** in Joseph and unto Judah a **choice vine**. *Jesus is that choice vine.* Now Jesus is speaking to His own, to eleven men, a very personal conversation. The crescendo of all history is about to take place, the crucifixion is about to occur within a matter of hours. He is walking between the upper room and the Garden of Gethsemane. He is telling them, "Remember the prophecy concerning Judah, the choice vine. I am that choice vine. I am the true vine and My Father is the husbandman. My Father planted Me."

In John 15:5 Jesus is making a special connection with His disciples. *"I am the vine, ye are the branches: He that abideth in me, and I in him, the same bringeth forth much fruit: for without me ye can do nothing."* He is saying to them, 'You are the branches. My Father planted the vine and the branches come out of the vine. You are a planting of God.' He was talking to men who were Israelites. You are part of the vine that was mentioned in Genesis 49 by our father Jacob. This is the choice vine. What does the word **choice** mean. It means growing the best of the grapes, deep purple, luscious grapes and that is what these eleven men were going to produce. 'This intimate spiritual organic relationship that you have with Me and I have with you, means that you are going to produce just as I have produced.' Now we too are part of what those eleven anointed disciples produced.

This vine is not given to husbandmen, plural, but to a husbandman, singular. That husbandman is the Heavenly Father. Husbandman, singular denotes a personal planting and personal care. Just as much as Jesus was given personal planting and care, we are given the same tender care, because we are organically connected to Jesus Christ. He is the vine and we are the branches. An integral part of us came out of Him because He, being the vine, is the life source of us as His branches.

This word *vine* in John 15 means 'a vine as though it were coiling about an arbor support.' Grape vines become very strong. They grow larger and larger. Even the smaller branches are strong because they have to hold up some weighty grapes. Therefore the tendrils coil around the supporting structure of the arbor. We are not only connected to the Vine, but we are supported by other branches. This word *true* means faithful, choice, special and the best. This Vine is the best of Israel, the best of the vineyard of the Lord. Jesus Christ is the best of the vineyard of the Lord and we have an organic spiritual connection with that particular vine of the vineyard. Jesus is that choice vine, that section of the vineyard cared for by the Heavenly Father and we are part of that particular Vine.

In Matthew 26:26 Jesus was reclining at the table and serving His disciples. Matthew records: *"And as they were eating, Jesus took bread, and blessed it, and brake it, and gave it to the disciples, and said, Take, eat; this is my body. And he took the cup* [the fruit of the vine], *and gave thanks, and gave it to them, saying, Drink ye all of it. For this is my blood of the new testament, which is shed for many for the remission of sins."*

At the last supper Jesus served them bread and wine. The wine comes from the fruit of the vine. John 6:32: *"Then Jesus said unto them, Verily, verily, I say unto you, Moses gave you not that bread from heaven; but my Father giveth you the true bread from heaven."* We know that a true vine produces a true wine and now we have a true bread as well. What did Melchizedek serve Abram. Bread and wine. Jesus said, I am the true Bread from Heaven. Then He gives another definition in verse 33, where He says, the bread of

God: *"For the bread of God is he which cometh down from heaven, and giveth life unto the world."* Did He say the bread of God was a 'thing'. No, He said the bread of God is **He,** referring to Himself. Verse 35, *"And Jesus said unto them, I am the bread of life: he that cometh to me shall never hunger; and he that believeth on me shall never thirst."* Then He said in verse 48, *"I am that bread of life."* I am the source of your strength. **Bread** denotes strength, food and sustenance. **Wine** denotes joy and lifegiving. Bread and wine is what Melchizedek served and what Jesus served and now He is declaring to His disciples: "I am the **True Vine**. I am the **True Bread**. I am the **Choice Vine**. I am the one who will produce the deep purple, luscious grapes."

John 6:51: *"I am the living bread which came down from heaven: if any man eat of this bread, he shall live for ever: and the bread that I will give is my flesh, which I will give for the life of the world."* Verse 53, *"Then Jesus said unto them, Verily, verily, I say unto you, Except ye eat the flesh of the Son of man, and drink his blood,* [represented by wine. *ye have no life in you. Whoso eateth my flesh, and drinketh my blood,* [He puts them together.] *hath eternal life; and I will raise him up at the last day. For my flesh is meat indeed, and my blood is drink indeed. He that eateth my flesh, and drinketh my blood, dwelleth in me, and I in him."* That is our connection. His spiritual body and His blood we consume, because we are connected to the vine and we eat the spiritual bread that came down from heaven. That is Jesus.

Melchizedek is not only **serving** the bread and wine, He **becomes** the bread and wine. That is why He could say 'eat my flesh and drink my blood.' How much closer connection could we have with Him spiritually. He called Himself the true bread, bread of life, bread from heaven and living bread. *Bread* is spiritual life and salvation. *Wine* represents joy, which is the infilling of the Holy Spirit. Do we need to be filled with the Holy Spirit only one time. When you are thirsty you drink water and then you drink more water. The Holy Spirit provides a continuous infilling, a relationship and an ongoing experience. We need more life, daily life, the infilling of the Spirit of God over and over again. What is the infilling of the Holy Spirit? *It is letting God be God within you.* It is not just speaking in tongues; it is letting God be God in you in every facet of life.

In Acts 2 the neighbors thought those 120 people were acting a little strange on the Day of Pentecost. They said, 'Those people must be drunk with *new wine.*' But that new wine was symbolic of the Spirit. When Jesus said "I am the vine" He was declaring it as the Melchizedek priest, the greatest symbol of connection and identification with His followers. "I am the vine, you are the branches. You are connected with Me. You are going to abide in Me and I am going to abide in you. You are going to eat My flesh and you are going to drink My blood. I served you bread and wine at the table, but there is something greater than eating just the symbol of My body. There is more than the symbol of drinking the cup of wine at Passover time. I am going to be the very life source that you must depend upon constantly every day of your life. You are going to eat My Word, and live in My Word. You are going to be consumed by My Word and drink of My Holy Spirit, and have life as no one has experienced it before. If you don't abide in Me, My Father will break off that branch." *Melchizedek is the bread and the wine*. Jesus wasn't just speaking as a man here; He was speaking as the God-man.

In I Corinthians 10:15 the Apostle Paul was writing these words approximately 28 years later. He said: *"I speak as to wise men; judge ye what I say. The cup of blessing which we bless, is it not the communion of the blood of Christ? The bread which we break, is it not the communion of the body of Christ?"* He did not say, 'Is it not the blood and body of Christ. He said, 'Is it not the **communion** of the body and blood of Christ?' Verse 17. *"For we being many are one bread, and one body: for we are all partakers of that one bread."* Are we not many. One vine, one body, yet all partakers of that same vine and of that same bread. This is one of the greatest discourses of our Lord, but is hidden in the obscurity of parabolic language.

Unless we know who we are this passage means nothing. Jesus did not pull a metaphor out of thin air when He said, 'I am the vine.' He knew what His forefather Jacob had said. This Choice Vine of Judah is going to be connected with Joseph the fruitful bough. Now the climax of all the ages was upon Him and His followers. The true vine is now beginning to grow. It is going to be planted and cared for by their Heavenly Father. Those of His body are the true vine of the vineyard of the Lord. The vineyard has grown over the wall. That fruitful bough filled the land and it went beyond the oceans and rivers, yet there was a Choice Vine among that vineyard that is cared for by our Heavenly Father. We are part of that vine because we are the branches.

Thank God for divine revelation. When the Holy Spirit comes He is not going to speak of Himself. He is going to speak of Jesus. He is going to take things that He has said and bring them to our remembrance. Your life source is the bread and wine that He serves. Thank God for the Levitical priesthood, but the Melchizedek priesthood is greater, because of it's greater communion and blessing. Let us enter into it with rejoicing!

Now do you see why one New Testament writer said the angels and the prophets desired to look into the things that we talk about today. They wait for us to join them in Glory because they cannot be perfected without us.

SHEM – THE THIRD GENERATION FROM ADAM BY WAY OF MOUTH

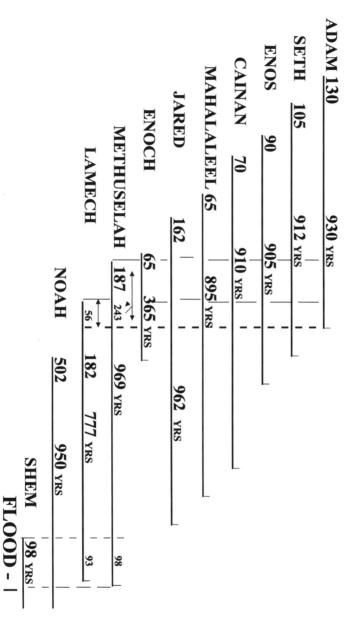

ADAM 130 — 930 YRS

SETH 105 — 912 YRS

ENOS 90 — 905 YRS

CAINAN 70 — 910 YRS

MAHALALEEL 65 — 895 YRS

JARED 162 — 962 YRS

ENOCH 65 — 365 YRS

METHUSELAH 187 — 969 YRS

LAMECH 182 — 777 YRS

243

56

NOAH 502 — 950 YRS

93

98

SHEM

FLOOD – | 98 YRS |

WHO WAS MELCHIZEDEK?

Gen. 14:17-20

The following information and chart shows that Shem was still living at the time when Abram met Melchizedek.

Gen. 11:10	Shem	was 100 years old when his son was born
Gen. 11:12	Arphaxad	was 35 years old when his son was born
Gen. 11:14	Salah	was 30 years old when his son was born
Gen. 11:16	Eber	was 34 years old when his son was born
Gen. 11:18	Peleg	was 30 years old when his son was born
Gen. 11:20	Reu	was 32 years old when his son was born
Gen. 11:22	Serug	was 30 years old when his son was born
Gen. 11:24	Nabor	was 29 years old when his son was born
Gen. 11:26	Terah	was 70 years old when his son was born
		390

Shem was 390 years old when Abram was born and lived another 210 years, which totaled 600 years. Abram only lived 175 years (Gen. 25:7) therefore, Shem outlived Abram by 35 years.

```
                    FLOOD
                      |
NOAH 600 YEARS        | 350 YRS= 950 YRS  (GEN. 9:28-29)
_____|_____
                      |
SHEM 98               |  2 |  290  |   75   |  100  | 35 = 600YRS
_____|____|_____|_____|_____|_____
                     ↗          | GEN.14:18 |
              GEN. 11:10        | ABRAM 75 | 100 | = 175 YRS
                                   Gen. 12:4
```

ISAAC BORN - ABRAHAM 100 YRS. OLD - Genesis 21:5

JACOB BORN - ABRAHAM 160 YRS OLD - Genesis 25:26

ISAAC WAS 110 YEARS OLD WHEN SHEM DIES
JACOB WAS 50 YEARS OLD WHEN SHEM DIED
ABRAHAM'S GREAT GRANDSON LEVI, BORN 172 YEARS
AFTER GENESIS 14:18-20

A-2

WHO WAS MELCHIZEDEK?

REASONS TO BELIEVE THAT SHEM WAS MELCHIZEDEK

1. Shem was definitely mentioned in conjunction with Noah's blessing of the LORD (Gen. 9:26) and therefore implies that Shem was a devout and Godly man and consequently had a blessing conferred upon him.

2. Shem was still alive at the time Abram met Melchizedek (as shown by the chart on page 177). **Shem** was his *earthly* name and **Melchizedek** was his *priestly* and *kingly* name.

SIMILARITIES OF MELCHIZEDEK AND CHRIST
HEBREWS 7:1-21

1. Neither one was from the tribe of Levi - Hebrews 7:14

2. Both had a continuing priesthood - Hebrews 7 :24

3. Both were appointed priests by oath and not by the law of commandment or ancestral descent Hebrews 5:6; 7:17, 20-21

4. The Melchizedek Priesthood was the order which was already in place that Christ had to meet qualifications for or otherwise He was not "after the order of" Melchizedek, and would therefore have been establishing His own order of Priesthood.

5. In John 8:56-58 Christ stated that Abraham saw "My day"; that is Christ's day or the dual King-Priest office of Christ as exhibited in Melchizedek as recorded in Genesis 14:17-20.

PRINCIPLES THAT WERE HIGHLY RESPECTED IN OLD TESTAMENT TIMES

1. *FATHERHOOD* -- The oldest living patriarch of the Adamic race at any given time was considered to be the ***civil authority*** of his race or ***KING***.

2. *PRIESTHOOD* -- The oldest living patriarch of the Adamic race at any given time was considered to be the ***religious authority*** of his race or ***PRIEST***.

JESUS CHRIST AS MELCHIZEDEK

The writer of the book of Hebrews draws a comparison between the Melchizedek order and Levitical order of priesthoods. The Levitical order was fulfilled by Jesus during the days of His flesh when He paid the sacrificial offering for sin. The anointing of the Levitical priesthood is forever in order to deal with the problem of sin, its consequences and the principle of divine forgiveness (Ex. 40:15; Jer. 33:18).

The Melchizedek priesthood finds its complete fulfillment only in the person and work of Jesus Christ. It also was first in time and superior in rank. All Scripture references below are from the book of Hebrews.

THE CONTRAST OF PRIESTHOODS

The Order of Melchizedek	The Order of Levi
Received tithes 7:2,4,6,9	Paid tithes 7:9
Not by descent 7:3,6,15,16	By descent 7:5, 16
Tribe of Judah 7: 14	Tribe of Levi 7:5, 11
Office conferred by oath 7: 17, 20, 21	No oath 7:21
Endless life 7:8, 16, 25	Death 7:8, 23
Blesses - serves bread and wine 7:6-7; Matt. 26:26-28 John 6:53	Administered the Law 7: 11
One Priest 7:24	Many priests 7:21, 23, 27
Office of Priesthood is forever 7:21, 25	Temporary Priesthood 7:23
Unchangeable Priesthood 7:24	Changeable Priesthood 7:11-12
Perfect Priest 7:11, 19	Imperfect Priests 7:11, 19
No sacrifice needed for Himself 7:26-27	Sacrifice needed for himself 7:27
One Sacrifice 7:27; 9:12	Daily sacrifice 7:27
Offered Himself 7:27	Animal sacrifices 9:12-13
Consecrated forever 7:28; five fold 7:26 - holy, harmless, undefiled separate from sinner and made higher	Had infirmities 7:28

The fulfillment of the Melchizedek Order is now only in Christ Jesus Heb. 6:19-20

Jesus fulfills the dual office of both King and Priest Zech 6:9-13; Rev. 5:5-6

THE TWO PRIESTHOODS

ROYAL PRIESTHOOD OF MELCHISEDEC

CARNAL PRIESTHOOD OF LEVI

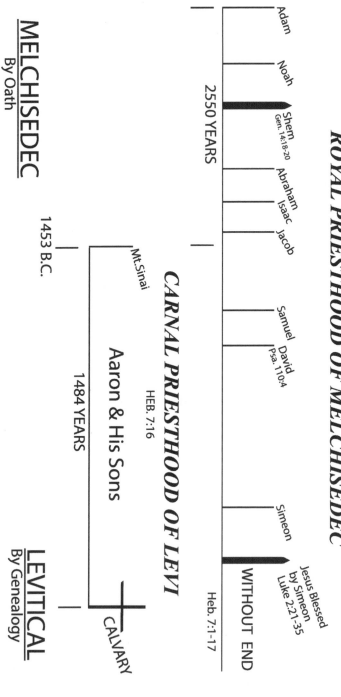

MELCHISEDEC
By Oath

LEVITICAL
By Genealogy

Adam

Noah

Shem
Gen. 14:18-20

Abraham

Isaac

Jacob

Samuel

David
Psa. 110:4

Simeon

2550 YEARS

1453 B.C.

Mt.Sinai

Aaron & His Sons

HEB. 7:16

1484 YEARS

CALVARY

Jesus Blessed
by Simeon
Luke 2:21-35

WITHOUT END

Heb. 7:1-17

A-6

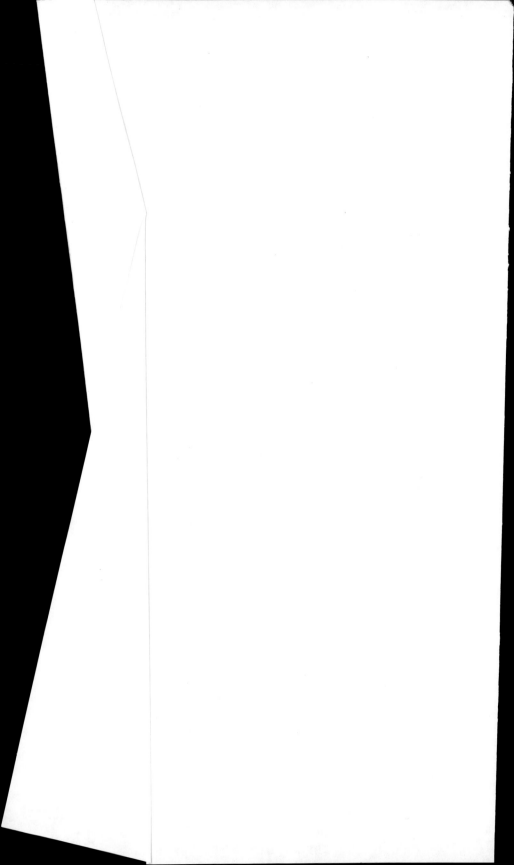

Made in the USA
Columbia, SC
25 May 2022

60805762R00115